History of Brazil

A Captivating Guide to Brazilian History, Starting from the Ancient Marajoara Civilization through Colonization by the Portuguese Empire to the Present

© Copyright 2021

All Rights Reserved. No part of this book may be reproduced in any form without permission in writing from the author. Reviewers may quote brief passages in reviews.

Disclaimer: No part of this publication may be reproduced or transmitted in any form or by any means, mechanical or electronic, including photocopying or recording, or by any information storage and retrieval system, or transmitted by email without permission in writing from the publisher.

While all attempts have been made to verify the information provided in this publication, neither the author nor the publisher assumes any responsibility for errors, omissions or contrary interpretations of the subject matter herein.

This book is for entertainment purposes only. The views expressed are those of the author alone, and should not be taken as expert instruction or commands. The reader is responsible for his or her own actions.

Adherence to all applicable laws and regulations, including international, federal, state and local laws governing professional licensing, business practices, advertising and all other aspects of doing business in the US, Canada, UK or any other jurisdiction is the sole responsibility of the purchaser or reader.

Neither the author nor the publisher assumes any responsibility or liability whatsoever on the behalf of the purchaser or reader of these materials. Any perceived slight of any individual or organization is purely unintentional.

Free Bonus from Captivating History (Available for a Limited time)

Hi History Lovers!

Now you have a chance to join our exclusive history list so you can get your first history ebook for free as well as discounts and a potential to get more history books for free! Simply visit the link below to join.

Captivatinghistory.com/ebook

Also, make sure to follow us on Facebook, Twitter and Youtube by searching for Captivating History.

Table of Contents

INTRODUCTION 1
CHAPTER 1 - BRAZIL'S FIRST HUMANS AND DEVELOPMENT PRE-EUROPEAN CONTACT (UNKNOWN-1532) 3
CHAPTER 2 - PORTUGAL CLAIMS BRAZIL (1494-1535) 14
CHAPTER 3 - PORTUGAL'S FIRST SETTLEMENTS IN BRAZIL AND THE EARLY YEARS IN THE CAPTAINCIES (1533-1580) 19
CHAPTER 4 - THE IBERIAN UNION, NIEUW HOLLAND, AND THE PORTUGUESE RESTORATION WAR (1580-1668) 28
CHAPTER 5 - EXPLORATION AND BRAZIL'S GOLD AND DIAMOND RUSH (1668-1800) 37
CHAPTER 6 - THE PORTUGUESE COURT IN BRAZIL, THE FORMATION OF BRAZIL'S MONARCHY, AND INDEPENDENCE FROM PORTUGAL (1800-1822) 53
CHAPTER 7 - BRAZIL'S FIRST INDEPENDENT EMPIRE UNDER PEDRO I (1822-1831) 58
CHAPTER 8 - BRAZIL'S REGENCY PERIOD, THE EMPIRE OF PEDRO II, AND THE COLLAPSE OF BRAZIL'S MONARCHY (1831-1889) 69
CHAPTER 9 - THE FORMATION AND DEVELOPMENT OF THE BRAZILIAN REPUBLIC IN THE LATE 19TH AND EARLY 20TH CENTURIES (1889-1950) 86
CHAPTER 10 - BRAZIL IN THE SECOND HALF OF THE 20TH CENTURY (1950-2000) 97
CONCLUSION 104
HERE'S ANOTHER BOOK BY CAPTIVATING HISTORY THAT YOU MIGHT LIKE 106
FREE BONUS FROM CAPTIVATING HISTORY (AVAILABLE FOR A LIMITED TIME) 107
BIBLIOGRAPHY 108

Introduction

How did Brazil go from a land that was deemed unprofitable and uninhabitable to one of the countries with the highest GDPs and populations in the world?

Brazil has a rich and convoluted history that is made more complicated by the fact that so much of it is unknown. This is especially true for its history before European contact, although evidence reveals indigenous tribes may have reached unprecedented levels of modernization. Though Portugal quickly claimed the land as its own during the European race for colonization, many explorers felt Brazil would not be worth the time and investment necessary to colonize. Unlike its neighboring American territories, it went mostly undeveloped until the start of the sugar industry.

While some nations' histories can be entirely tied to wars or immigration booms, Brazil's modern history is completely attached to its economy. Though it now has an extremely diversified income, until recently, Brazil almost entirely focused its society and economy on one product at a time. The sugar industry developed its first cities and created the world's biggest slave trade. The gold rush led to the exploration and development of Brazil's interior. The coffee industry ended up making its way into politics, as most of Brazil's first presidents (the coffee presidents) were directly involved in coffee production.

Yet, despite being a nation so centered around its economy and so focused on its reputation early on, Brazil is not considered a powerhouse nation. Brazil spent most of its recent history in an economic crisis known for bringing poverty, inflation, and financial disparity.

Unlike other neighboring countries, which had to fight for their independence from their colonizers, Brazil experienced little turmoil on its road to liberation. During the Napoleonic Wars, the Portuguese monarchy fled to Rio de Janeiro, where the heir to the Portuguese throne lived, claiming Brazil as an independent empire of Portugal.

Despite not needing to fight many revolutionary, destructive battles early on, most of the 20th century in Brazil would be marked by uprisings. Why have Brazilians spent the majority of recent history dissatisfied with their politicians, and why is Brazil so impoverished despite its growing economic importance worldwide? Let's explore more of Brazil's history to better understand its situation today.

Chapter 1 – Brazil's First Humans and Development Pre-European Contact (Unknown–1532)

Origins of America's First People

As with the prehistories of most nations, little is known for sure about Brazil's prehistoric period, and nothing that is known is agreed upon or certain. That being said, most historians agree that America's first people were hunter-gatherers who came from Asia. They crossed a no-longer existent land bridge in the Bering Strait. Since prehistoric prey was so large and tools were primal, hunter-gatherer groups stalked their prey for weeks before catching it, following it as it traveled dozens, if not hundreds, of kilometers. Historians theorize hunters followed their prey from the northeastern tip of Russia to the northwestern tip of Alaska, which, at its shortest distance, is around ninety kilometers away.

While this is the most commonly accepted theory of how the first people arrived in America, the discovery of identical tools in both America and Europe has led some archaeologists to believe that America's first people actually crossed ice packs through the Atlantic. Some indigenous populations of America believe their ancestors never migrated at all. Nonetheless, most evidence seems to point toward people crossing the Pacific and coming from Asia. However, that is where the majority of historians, scientists, archaeologists, and anthropologists seem to branch off.

Estimated Time of Arrival

One of the most contentious elements of Brazil's prehistoric history is when the first people arrived in the Americas. The estimated time of arrival keeps moving further and further from today as more evidence is found. For decades, it was believed the first humans arrived in the Americas around thirteen thousand years ago and reached Brazil around nine thousand years ago. There have since been many archaeological discoveries that have pushed both dates further back, one of which being the uncovering of Serra da Capivara National Park.

In the 1970s, scientists were exploring the forests of northeastern Brazil when they discovered red ochre paintings on rock formations that were covered in flowering plants. Among the typical battle scenes, which depict hunters carrying spears, were cave paintings of people standing alongside animals. Over the years, experts uncovered thousands of rock paintings, stone tools, and other evidence of prehistoric human existence. Since Serra da Capivara is so large (around one and a half times the acreage of the five boroughs of New York), the site is now considered to be the largest concentration of prehistoric sites in the Americas.

The evidence discovered in the Serra da Capivara archaeological sites was tested and proven to be over nine thousand years old, which challenged the original belief of when humans first arrived in Brazil. Skulls discovered in the region were estimated to be at least eleven thousand years old, and some of the stone tools have even been dated to twenty-two thousand years old. Assuming the first people of the Americas did hail from Asia and cross over the Bering Strait to Alaska and then eventually spread east and southward, people would have arrived in the Americas long before the previously estimated date.

After more evidence was discovered at Serra da Capivara, corroborating the dating of Brazil's first people to over twenty thousand years ago, some historians and scientists formed new theories. Nièvre Guidon, a Brazilian archaeologist who helped lead the excavations in the Serra da Capivara archaeological site, claimed that almost twenty years before working at Serra da Capivara, she and her team found evidence that proves humans were in Brazil forty-eight thousand years ago. After compiling all of her research, Guidon believed that humans may have even been in Brazil around 100,000 years ago. This would mean there were humans in Brazil long before the rest of the Americas. Guidon formed a theory that indigenous Brazilians were not ancestors of Asians who crossed the Bering Strait but were instead ancestors of Africans who crossed the Atlantic Ocean by boat.

While Guidon is not alone in thinking this, most historians disagree with her. Some scientists believe the evidence proving human existence over forty thousand years ago actually proved the existence of monkeys, who have been proven to have lived in Brazil for over thirty million years. Currently, Brazil's prehistory is wrapped up in mysteries and debates. As more archaeological sites are discovered, we are able to develop a better understanding of the first humans in the country. It is likely that within a decade or two, Brazil's prehistory will be entirely different than it is known today.

What complicates our understanding of the origin of Brazil's first humans is the fact that there were likely many waves of immigrants. Furthermore, the region's acidic soil and humid climate are not conducive to preservation. Most human and animal bones, wooden structures, and wooden tools have been destroyed by nature at a far more rapid rate than in other parts of the Americas. What little was not destroyed over the course of many millennia has shaped the limited understanding we have of the prehistoric humans of Brazil.

Paleolithic and Mesolithic Cultures in Brazil

Alongside the prehistoric paintings, most evidence proving the existence of prehistoric humans in Brazil is in the form of stone tools. The Lithic period, which refers to the Paleolithic (Old Stone Age), Mesolithic (Middle Stone Age), and Neolithic (New Stone Age) periods, occurred around eleven thousand years ago in Brazil. During that time, two main lithic (stone) cultures emerged. The first of these lithic cultures was the Uruguayan tradition, which was known for its stone knives, scrapers, picks, and weapons designed with two flat faces, a pointed tip, and a handle. The second prominent lithic culture in Brazil was the Itaparica tradition, which featured single-faced tools. The Itaparica culture is mostly known for producing the prehistoric rock and cave paintings archaeologists have discovered.

While both Itaparica and Uruguayan tools would have been carved from similar stones, the main difference between the two traditions is that the latter flaked both sides of the tools. Both varieties of tools were used for similar purposes: cutting, chopping, scraping, and carving. The slight differences in the tools help historians to understand that different cultures existed in prehistoric Brazil.

Neolithic Cultures

Around seven thousand years ago, most unifacial tools had been phased out. New cultures emerged, such as the Humaitá and the Sambaqui traditions, both of which used bifacial tools. The Humaitá culture mostly inhabited broadleaf forests. They did not use tipped tools but increased the size of their tools, making them larger than the ones used by the Uruguayan, Itaparica, and Sambaqui cultures. The Sambaqui culture mostly inhabited the southern coasts of Brazil and consumed a large number of shellfish. Shell middens, which are garbage piles, were discovered, which helped to confirm shellfish and other seafood as being an essential part of the Sambaqui people's diet.

There were some other smaller cultures inhabiting Brazil at the time, such as the Umbu tradition, which continued to use pointed tools and mostly inhabited the more open landscapes. Up until this point, it is believed that most cultures were nomadic or at least semi-nomadic.

Evidence discovered along the coastline of modern-day Rio de Janeiro and Espírito Santo suggests that some of the first permanent settlements were created around four thousand years ago. These sedentary groups were largely focused on agriculture and were known to grow not only practical crops for food or shelter purposes but also plants for aesthetic reasons, much like modern-day homeowners having floral gardens. Although agriculture was present in Brazil before this period, permanent settlements allowed groups to grow more time-intensive crops, such as trees, which could take years to produce fruit.

Agriculture was now under the care of not only one tribe for a short period but also a tribe's ancestors and future generations. The main crop grown by sedentary communities was maize or corn; however, most communities continued to hunt and gather. Another common crop likely grown by these farming communities was cassava, also known as yuca or sweet manioc.

Indigenous Populations before Year 0

Over the course of the next centuries, the indigenous populations developed into hundreds of tribes, each with its own culture, customs, systems, diets, beliefs, and living arrangements. Today, there are just over three hundred known tribes in Brazil, likely a third of which live completely isolated and uncontacted from the rest of society. There were most likely far more tribes before European contact, perhaps nearing even two thousand; however, the exact number is unknown. Despite all of the uniquely different groups in Brazil, the population would mostly be split into sedentary or semi-nomadic farming settlements and semi-nomadic hunter-gatherers. Farming communities that settled in areas with rich, fertile soil and had a separate sustainable source of food (such as a river for fishing) no longer had to migrate.

These permanent settlements were mostly located around the Andes Mountains, where settlements actually urbanized as tribes joined together. The most significant of these urbanized communities were located west of the Andes, outside of Brazil's present borders. Despite urbanizing in some ways, these permanent settlers never built any major structures that have lasted, which makes it difficult to truly unravel the history of Brazil.

East of the Andes, in less fertile regions, farming communities were forced to migrate on a seasonal basis. This instability led to warring between tribes, which fought over unclaimed lands. Farming communities that lived in regions with less fertile soil were known to use the slash-and-burn agriculture method, which refers to the burning of forests to improve soil quality to make space for crops. Around a decade after burning down the forest, farming communities returned to the site again, as the soil would be fertile once again. These communities usually planted crops repeatedly, which deteriorated the soil. They burned the plots, found new land, and repeated the process. Nowadays, advancements in agriculture have shown that crop rotation is extremely beneficial in preserving soil, as crops extract different nutrients from the soil. However, slash-and-burn is still recognized as a functional and sustainable soil fertilization technique, although less efficient than crop rotation.

Much like farming communities in poor soil regions, hunter-gathering communities were mostly semi-nomadic, settling in one area until resources ran out, which led to instability and wars. Communities warred over food and land, but there were also social disputes and resource disputes, such as the fight for the brazilwood tree's red dye. Although semi-nomadic Brazilian tribes struggled with agriculture, almost all of them were incredible hunters. According to European accounts, even young children were unbelievably accurate with shooting bows and arrows, rarely missing even the smallest and fastest of prey.

One practice used by some Brazilian tribes to gain an advantage in war and solve food scarcity was cannibalism. Cannibalism was used by some tribes as any other war tactic. Warring communities ambushed their enemy's communities. Instead of simply killing the leaders, they would make an example of the leaders by eating them. People who were intended to be consumed were exchanged as a way to end wars. Cannibalism was mostly used for revenge.

Regardless of why cannibalism was practiced, there were many rituals surrounding the process. Every tribe had its own traditions, which included how they treated the captive, how they were killed, how they were cooked, and how they were consumed.

While cannibalism might seem villainous by today's standards, it is far more ingrained in nature than most are aware of. Cannibalism is present among many animals and creatures, and while humans are classified as separate from the rest of the animal kingdom, prehistoric, semi-nomadic tribes were entirely focused on survival. Unlike the farming tribes, which focused on agriculture, had sustainable food sources, and had time to create political and social systems, semi-nomadic cultures were always thinking of food. In most parts of the world, sedentary settlements were strongly opposed to cannibalism, while struggling nomadic communities were less opposed to the practice. Since many indigenous tribes around the world believed themselves to be connected to nature and just as important as the animals and plants around them, it is no surprise that human life was considered similar to prey.

All of that being said, cannibalism was not only practiced by indigenous, semi-nomadic tribes. There is evidence of cannibalism in Europe until the 1800s, long after it was considered taboo. It would seem that no matter what one believes, when times get hard enough and food is scarce, many communities turn to cannibalism. There is even evidence of this in modern-day situations. Of course, that does not make the consummation of humans any less horrid to modern-day humans or sedentary civilians living in permanent societies.

As European nations began making contact with tribes around the world, cannibalism was the universal sign that a tribe should no longer be treated as humans. Even Christopher Columbus, who rediscovered the Americas, was instructed to be as "kind" as possible to native tribes unless they were cannibals. Today, historians doubt many of the reports of cannibalism made by the first Europeans in Brazil and other regions in the Americas. Once a group was labeled as cannibals, European nations felt no regret enslaving, murdering, and sexually assaulting the indigenous people. While this is not the case for all, as cannibalism was certainly practiced in Brazil and other parts of the world, it is likely some reports of cannibalism were faked so a country could colonize the region faster.

Indigenous Populations before European Contact

While nature's destruction of artifacts and buildings means that most of what we know about the indigenous tribes of Brazil comes from European accounts, some regions had better conditions for the preservation of artifacts than others. In the Marajó area, advanced pottery creations were discovered, dating to around one thousand to three thousand years ago. The pottery, which was advanced for its time and painted with patterns of detailed plants and animals, led archaeologists to invest more time in exploring the region. Upon further investigation, mounds large enough to fit entire villages were discovered. Although these platforms were originally thought to be for ceremonial purposes, further exploration led experts to believe the platforms were bases for large communities that lived permanently in longhouses built upon the mounds.

Shell middens were discovered that contained not only shellfish and fishbones but also seeds, rocks, and other items, indicating the existence of agriculture, fishing, gathering, and hunting. The surprising diversity in the community's diet led scientists to believe there was a sophisticated economy and trade market of sorts on Marajó Island. All of this evidence and other archaeological discoveries suggest that pre-European contact, there were communities with complex political, social, trade, and religious systems. While the exact population of the Marajoara culture is unknown, it is assumed there were thousands of people cohabiting by the time the Europeans arrived in Brazil.

As more archaeological sites are discovered around the country, the belief that ancient Brazil had advanced societies is gaining popularity among experts. When European adventurers first reached Brazil, they reported complex civilizations containing hundreds of thousands of people. For example, Spain's Gaspar de Carvajal wrote of Amazonian "cities that gleamed white" in the 1540s.

However, other than some century-old descriptions, there is very little concrete evidence of the civilizations being described. Much of what has been discovered can be disproven or simply be the work of nature rather than of humans. This might sound strange; how can nature look like something humans made? For example, according to anthropologist Augusto Oyuela-Caycedo, the Amazon has unusual clustering of fruit trees. This might be because of human agriculture, or the region simply might be fertile. Other historians argue that these small pieces of evidence may be proof of smaller civilizations. The theory that the Amazon once housed massive civilizations is hard to believe for most since the region is currently uninhabitable due to its dense plants and dangerous animals.

Over the centuries, many explorers set out to the Amazon in search of proof of these large civilizations. Some returned empty-handed, others reportedly lost their way or minds in the dense forests, and some disappeared completely, most notably Colonel Percy Fawcett. To avoid all of the negative outcomes those who came before him suffered, Michael Heckenberger from the University of Florida and his team of anthropologists gained the trust and friendship of the indigenous populations of that area, notably the Kuikuro, before setting out. This strategy turned out to be successful, and the team was able to uncover what appeared to be twenty-eight towns connected with bridges, roads, and canals. Some of the towns were even equipped with defensive ditches.

While some remains of structures remained, human occupation was proven through the tools and ceramic utensils that remained preserved for an estimated one thousand years. There is some evidence of large fields for agriculture and artificial ponds for fishing. The sheer size of the grouping of towns could easily inhabit at least fifty thousand people, which would align with Portuguese reports from the 1750s that spoke of tens of thousands of people living around the Xingu River. While the dates are controversial, it is believed these towns were inhabited from around 1,500 years to around 400 years ago when the Portuguese began making contact with and transferring diseases to the native Brazilians.

More proof of civilizations in pre-European Brazil are the presence of rock structures and geoglyphs. Geoglyphs refer to large-scale designs of natural materials, such as rocks, that form a massive image only visible from above. These geoglyphs have been dated to around two thousand to one thousand years ago, as has the rock formation that has been titled Brazil's Stonehenge.

A part of Brazil's Stonehenge.
Leandroisola, CC BY-SA 4.0 <https://creativecommons.org/licenses/by-sa/4.0>, via Wikimedia Commons;
https://commons.wikimedia.org/wiki/File:Cal%C3%A7oene,_Stonehenge_brasileira,_Amap%C3%A1.jpg

Brazil's history before European colonization is likely one of the most convoluted and debated out of all of the European colonies. As mentioned before, this is mostly because of nature. The climate, soil, and wildlife in the country are not ideal for the preservation of archaeological findings. So, unlike other American countries, the areas that are believed to have housed ancient civilizations have not been preserved. However, despite the lack of human occupancy, these areas are very much alive due to the unique flora and fauna in the region. The Amazon, which is now considered to be an untouched "paradise," has regrown, so the extent of nature's cover-up will not truly be understood for decades, if ever.

Most of what is known about Brazil's first people comes from their modern-day ancestors, untrustworthy reports from the Portuguese, and the very small amount of unreliable archaeological discoveries. We can assume that the numbers of indigenous people today were much larger before European contact. For example, there are 305 different tribes and around 900,000 indigenous people living in Brazil today. Before European colonization, there were estimated to be at least two thousand different tribes and perhaps millions of indigenous people. Groups were likely far more interconnected than we know, although each tribe had its own customs, lifestyles, and beliefs, making it difficult to truly understand how the first people lived since evidence and reports are grouped together. The picture of wild, primitive cannibals described in the past may have been true for some tribes; however, we are learning more about how advanced, civilized, and modern other tribes may have been long before the Europeans arrived.

Chapter 2 – Portugal Claims Brazil (1494–1535)

First European Discoveries of the Americas

As the Brazilian populations settled and developed their cultures, lifestyles, and beliefs, European countries gradually increased their understanding of the rest of the world. In the 1200s and 1300s, European explorers, most notably Italy's Marco Polo, focused on discovering Asia. After exploring China and Mongolia, European nations became aware of the exotic products that could be found throughout Asia, such as silks, spices, and tea. While the riches that could be found in Asia were certainly worth the trip, the known routes from Europe to Asia were extremely dangerous and eventually expensive due to Ottoman-imposed taxes.

Throughout the 15th century, European nations began searching for safer and cheaper routes to Asia. Since little was known for sure about geography at the time and since the existence of Australia and the Americas was still unknown, all routes were considered, including sailing around the southern tip of Africa and sailing west from Europe. This was how Christopher Columbus accidentally discovered the Americas.

Although he is rarely credited, Martín Alonso Pinzón (along with his brother, Vicente Yáñez Pinzónone), one of the commanders on Christopher Columbus's expedition to the Americas, is believed to have discovered Brazil. After exploring with Columbus in 1492,

Pinzón broke off to explore the surrounding lands. During this time, he is believed to have sailed the Amazon River, thereby discovering Brazil without actually claiming it for Spain.

Pinzón is not the only explorer historians believe may have visited Brazil before it was officially claimed for Portugal. For example, Portuguese explorer, Duarte Pacheco Pereira, described the land he visited, assumed now to be Brazil, in a book of his travels.

Portugal Receives Brazil in the Treaty of Tordesillas

Despite the fact that most of the powerful European countries had still not visited the Americas by 1494, there was increased interest in acquiring land in what came to be known as the "New World." Spain and Portugal had vested interests in what is now South America. Rather than warring over the land, the governments of Spain and Portugal instead met in the Spanish city of Tordesillas to decide how to divide the territory. The borders were drawn from north to south. The first crossed through Greenland and the eastern coast of South America, and the second line crossed eastern Russia to eastern Australia. Spain laid claim to most of the Americas and eastern Australia, while Portugal claimed all of Africa, the west of Australia, and, of course, the eastern coast of South America, which was Brazil.

Overall, the agreement, which is known as the Treaty of Tordesillas, was peaceful but not permanent. In 1506, the borders would be slightly adjusted so that Portugal could claim more of the eastern edge of South America to enlarge the territory of Brazil. Of course, Spain and Portugal were not the only ones that had an interest in claiming land in the New World, but at this time, no other European nation had visited the Americas. Within a few decades, this would change drastically, as the race to claim land abroad sped up. As soon as the Treaty of Tordesillas was agreed upon, both nations started planning expeditions to the Americas.

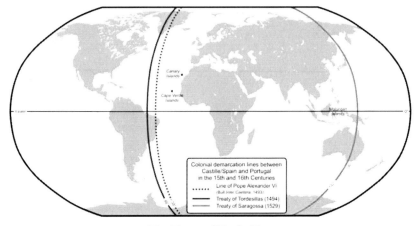

The Treaty of Tordesillas.
Lencer, CC BY-SA 3.0 <http://creativecommons.org/licenses/by-sa/3.0/>, via Wikimedia Commons; https://commons.wikimedia.org/wiki/File:Spain_and_Portugal.png

In 1498, Portuguese explorer Vasco da Gama successfully sailed from South Africa to India, and two years later, Pedro Álvares Cabral, another Portuguese explorer, attempted to replicate his journey. In 1500, Cabral was assigned the responsibility of leading an expedition of thirteen ships along Vasco da Gama's route to India. Portugal's king at the time, Manuel I, also instructed Cabral to forge trade relations with India upon his arrival.

To ensure Cabral reached his intended destination, Vasco da Gama left detailed directions that said Cabral should sail southwest rather than east once he arrived at the Gulf of Guinea, which is the part of the Atlantic Ocean that runs along the northeasternmost coast of Africa. This was not how da Gama originally sailed; however, it was believed to be the better route since the Gulf of Guinea was known to have unsuitable sailing conditions. Cabral adjusted his course slightly to the west, but slight changes in sailing can make huge differences. This adjustment caused Cabral and his ships to land on the coast of Porto Seguro in present-day Brazil. Thus, Cabral is credited with the discovery of Brazil, as he claimed the land for Portugal and named it Ilha de Vera Cruz, or Island of the True Cross. The original name is believed to have been inspired by the celebration of the Christian Feast of the Cross, which was celebrated in 1500 around the day of Brazil's discovery, which was in late April to early May.

Since Cabral was assigned to lead his expedition to India, not the Americas, the team only remained in Brazil for less than a week before continuing to India. However, in that short time, they tried to get a grasp of the people and landscape. In letters to Portugal, Cabral described peaceful contact with an indigenous tribe in Brazil that wore no clothes, slept in hammocks, and crafted bows and arrows for hunting.

First Two Decades of Portuguese Contact in Brazil

Portugal had little interest in settling in Brazil, unlike Spain, which colonized most of South America. Portugal also had little interest in evangelization, converting, or enslaving Brazilian natives, at least at first. Unlike in Asia, Portugal did not seek large-scale trade relations with the people of Brazil.

In the immediate years following Cabral's discovery, Portugal sponsored many expeditions to Brazil, which helped to map the coasts. However, after two decades, trade with Asia became more worthwhile than exploring Brazil, which had still not revealed any lucrative products. At this time, most of the Portuguese who arrived in Brazil were poor sailors searching for exotic goods that could help their financial situation back in Portugal. These first Portuguese contacts discovered little that could be financially worth something in Brazil, so they developed small-scale trade relations with some tribes, mostly to receive pau do brasil (brazilwood), which could be used to create red dye.

Unlike other parts of South America, Brazil, at least according to the Portuguese, had few major communities, such as the complex stone cities in the Andes. This meant the early European contacts were dealing with smaller tribes, making it easy to maintain peace. When small-scale battles occurred, they were over quickly because there weren't enough people to maintain long periods of warfare. Portugal's first impressions of the Brazilian natives were that they were overall harmless. They were complacent to alliances, peaceful with trade, and likely would be easy to convert to Catholicism.

Since Portugal put little effort into maintaining its claim of Brazil, French merchants created trade relations with tribes for brazilwood. As demand for brazilwood increased, the land became known as Terra do Brasil ("Land of Brazil"). In 1516, Portugal's king, Manuel I, officially referred to the land as Brazil. After the throne was passed to Manuel I's son, John III, the monarchy had a renewed interest in Brazil, likely due to the growing interest in Brazil from French merchants and the discoveries of profitable resources made by other European nations in the rest of the Americas.

Chapter 3 – Portugal's First Settlements in Brazil and the Early Years in the Captaincies (1533–1580)

Portugal's First Colonization Efforts in Brazil

Although one of the first Portuguese letters describing Brazil, written in 1500 by Pêro Vaz de Caminha, mentioned that "The country is so well-favoured that if it were rightly cultivated it would yield everything," Portugal was slow in creating settlements. Gradually, small trading posts were created along the coast of Brazil to encourage trade between the Portuguese merchants and the native populations. However, nothing major was established for a few decades. As other European nations, mainly France, became more interested in the resources available in Brazil, Portugal had no choice but to speed up its colonization if it wanted to keep its South American landmass. This, coupled with the fact that, around 1530, Portugal was searching for a new source of income since trade with Asian countries became less lucrative, forced Portugal to change its relaxed attitude toward Brazil.

In 1533, the first formal efforts were made to colonize, settle, and form a government in Brazil. King John III of Portugal granted land along the Brazilian coast to well-respected Portuguese nobles, who were known as *donatários*. The king first gave out fifteen land grants, which were known as captaincies. Each one was around 260 kilometers and located along the coast and as far inland as the landowner could maintain.

Most of the first landowners struggled greatly with maintaining their land. They were unfamiliar with the tropical climate and soil type, so they were unprepared to deal with the native population, who were displeased with their new neighbors expanding on their land. Of the first fifteen captaincies, only two ended up being successful: Pernambuco and São Vicente.

São Vicente

São Vicente, founded in 1532, is recognized as Brazil's first permanent Portuguese settlement. The *donatário* who established the settlement was Martim Afonso de Sousa, who was one of the admirals commanding the colonizing expedition to Brazil in the 1530s. Sousa quickly established a small government and economic system to encourage trade between the local population and the new settlers. Unlike a majority of the other landowners, who focused mainly on their new settlers, Sousa focused on forming peaceful relations with the native population, who were referred to as Indians.

Since the discovery of Brazil, missionaries had been requesting to visit the land to begin converting the population. The establishment of São Vicente gave the Jesuit Order their first chance to do so. The Jesuit Order played a huge role in the development of São Vicente, as its members quickly helped to construct churches for the settlers and missions and schools for the nearby tribes. While Portuguese reports may be biased, the missionaries of São Vicente were known to be gentler with the tribes than European colonizers had been in other parts of the continent. The Jesuit Order in São Vicente was actually known for being completely opposed to the slavery of the local "Indians," and they spoke out against slavery in other early settlements as well.

Sousa was recognized as a fair leader, which is likely why his settlement survived when most didn't. A while after Sousa established São Vicente, Spanish sailors shipwrecked near the settlement. Sousa's temperament led them to inform him of lucrative metals they had discovered within Brazil. Until the discovery of gold and silver, the captaincy of São Vicente struggled to keep up with the surrounding regions, which were developing sugarcane markets.

To survive and make a profit, in the mid-16th century, settlers began cultivating large stretches of untamed lands and planting wheat fields. Since São Vicente's products were not as lucrative as the other captaincies, it was not granted as many slaves. And to keep up with demand, they were eventually forced to go against the original Jesuit Order's beliefs and enforce slave labor. The Portuguese who "hunted" slaves in Brazil were known as the Bandeirantes, a position that would become more necessary in the following century.

In 1554, São Paulo was founded as the first highland settlement in Brazil. It was located in the extremely fertile Piratininga Plateau region. Since there was already an indigenous settlement there, Portuguese missionaries began constructing missions, churches, and schools. The population of São Paulo grew slowly, but it would eventually become an important base for the Bandeirantes' expeditions.

Pernambuco

The other early captaincies that were successful besides São Vicente was Pernambuco, which began in the city of Olinda in 1535. The *donatário* of that captaincy was Duarte Coelho Pereira, who earned his reputation by making great strides in forming trade relations with Asian nations, mainly India. During his time forming lucrative trade deals for Portugal, he amassed a small fortune of his own. Upon returning home to Portugal, he was recognized as a nobleman. After another decade, during which he led an armada in various regions of Africa, Pereira was assigned a captaincy in Brazil. His wealth and understanding of foreign relations helped him build a thriving community early on.

Pereira was given the most sought-after captaincy in Brazil, as it had fertile soil and was located on the easternmost tip of the landmass, meaning it was easiest to reach from Portugal. Upon their arrival, the new settlers were threatened by the native population, who did not want to share the land they had inhabited for generations. Wars continued for around two years until the

Portuguese emerged victorious.

While the brazilwood tree, which had already amassed a great demand back in Europe, was profitable for the early captaincy, *donatários* were constantly searching for lucrative products and experimenting with new crops that could increase profits. Although it's not known exactly when it began, around the late 1530s, Duarte Coelho Pereira's captaincy discovered what would eventually become one of the most lucrative exports for Brazil: sugarcane. By 1540, the settlement had fields of sugarcane, and a sugar mill had begun construction. Two years later, the sugar industry of Pernambuco was about to take off.

As the market for sugar skyrocketed, Pereira began requesting that Portugal send slaves to Brazil to keep up with demand, as did the other captaincies that followed Pernambuco's example and began planting sugarcane. Within less than a decade, Pernambuco alone had five working sugar mills, which were known as *engenhos*, and many more were being built.

Captaincies used Pernambuco as an example of how to generate wealth. Bahia, for example, which had been established in 1549, closely paralleled the sugarcane development in Pernambuco and grew its own lucrative market. Eventually, the captaincies that developed sugar markets left all those that had struggled to grow sugarcane or had attempted to go in a different direction in the dust, including São Vicente.

Duarte Coelho Pereira passed away sometime around 1553 when he returned to Portugal to argue with the king's plan to reduce the *donatários*' power, cut back on the land grant programs, and increase royal control in Brazil. Pereira's captaincy was left to his two sons, who would continue to grow the sugarcane market. Olinda, the first major city in Pernambuco, became the heart of the Portuguese economy in Brazil, and its population grew rapidly with its wealth. By the 1550s, the captaincies of São Vicente and Pernambuco had a combined population of approximately five thousand people. While this number was quite large for new settlements at the time, the Portuguese population of Brazil paled in comparison to the estimated three million indigenous Brazilians with whom they "shared" their land.

Systematic Changes in the Second Half of the 16ᵗʰ Century

Regardless of what Duarte Coelho Pereira and most of the other *donatários* wanted, King John III was insistent on following through with his plan to create a central government that would help to unify the captaincies. This change was necessary to help the struggling captaincies, many of which were nearing complete failure. These failing captaincies were more of a hindrance to the already succeeding captaincies, which would be forced to stop being solely self-interested and begin to help their struggling neighbors. King John III named Tomé de Sousa as governor-general of Brazil.

Tomé de Sousa's Initial Objectives as Brazil's First Governor-General

Similar to many of the *donatários*, Tomé de Sousa was a Portuguese noble who had extensive military experience in both Africa and India, which earned him an impressive reputation. Unlike the *donatários*, who were previously able to act more independently, Sousa was under the direct authority of the king of Portugal and was required to fulfill the king's wishes. In 1549, Sousa landed in Brazil alongside approximately one thousand others who accompanied him on his expedition, ranging from soldiers and priests to craftspeople.

Upon landing in Brazil, Sousa instantly fulfilled one of King John III's instructions, which was to establish the capital city of Salvador in the central captaincy of Bahia. Of course, since the captaincies were actually owned by their *donatários*, to create the capital city, Sousa had to buy the land within the captaincy of Bahia from its *donatário*, Francisco Pereira Coutinho. Salvador would remain the capital city of Brazil for 214 years until it was changed to Rio de Janeiro and then, more recently in the 20ᵗʰ century, Brasília.

Salvador was meant to represent the unification of the captaincies. It would act as a centralized city to govern what had previously been self-governed plots of land. Since many of the captaincies were almost as large, if not larger, than Portugal itself, Sousa sent soldiers and trusted officials to each of the capacitances to help maintain order and relay instructions. After ensuring Salvador was stable, Sousa traveled between the captaincies to help stabilize the struggling settlements. While visiting a captaincy, Sousa laid down new laws, established a government led by the officials and soldiers he had sent to govern the region, and expelled the more "hostile" natives with whom the Portuguese settlers had previously been sharing their land. The latter was often accomplished through violent wars, which were harmful to what was known as the "Indian" population of Brazil. Indigenous populations who were less combative and seemed as if they'd be easier to convert were allowed to remain within the captaincy.

Sousa had a few other initial objectives besides unifying the captaincies, aiding in the recovery of the struggling captaincies, and establishing the capital city of Salvador. First, Sousa was to defend Brazil's captaincies from pirates, who stole resources from the land. Since Portugal paid little attention to Brazil until the mid-16th century, piracy, specifically from French pirates, continued without consequences, but King John III instructed that Sousa change that. To defend Brazil, Sousa placed soldiers all along the coast and strategically fortified locations that needed better protection.

The next objective King John III instructed Sousa to carry out was to evangelize the indigenous population. As with most colonizing done by European nations at the time, converting the local population to Christianity became one of Portugal's main focuses in Brazil. After decades of requests from the Portuguese churches, in 1549, on the same expedition that brought Sousa, the first missionaries arrived in Brazil. The Jesuit mission was led by Father Manuel da Nóbrega, who was sent to Brazil with his own list of instructions from King John III. Father Nóbrega was to help build and develop Brazil and focus on educating and evangelizing the local population to increase Portugal's power.

The initial strategy to fulfill the king's wishes was to forcefully recruit the native tribes as laborers to help construct churches, tend to crops, and develop settlements. While being forced to work, the "Indians" would be forced to live in villages, known as aldeias, which were run by the Jesuits. They also had to attend conversion courses and church. The indigenous could only move to the aldeias after they converted, as the Jesuits believed they would no longer be hostile. To make the conversion process smoother, Jesuits learned Tupi, which was one of the most commonly understood languages among the indigenous populations who lived near the early Portuguese settlements.

As the Jesuits began finding success with converting the nearby tribes, the missions began extending farther from the settlements throughout interior Brazil. Over the next decade, as the missions continued, the native people living within the Portuguese settlements of Brazil lived as slaves. Indigenous people worked not only in the sugar industry, which was rapidly growing in the second half of the 16th century, but also on cattle ranches and cotton fields. This meant that within a decade, the indigenous population was helping to sustain most of Portugal's profitable exports and almost all of the food and clothing for the Portuguese settlers within Brazil. By the end of the 1550s, sugar production was almost equally run by elite businessmen and the Society of Jesus.

The Portuguese Crown, which wanted to export as much sugar as cheaply as possible, was not willing to employ settlers to work in the sugar industry. Before long, every landowner in Brazil wanted their own indigenous slaves to work on their plantations. The Jesuits quickly began petitioning the Crown to prevent this. This petition was not because they cared for the well-being of the natives but because they did not want to have to compete for labor. Louis-François de Tollenare, who was a French cotton buyer who often visited Pernambuco, was quoted as saying the slaves (both the natives and Africans) were equivalent to cattle, which perfectly explained the European view of the native population of Brazil at the time.

As demand for slave labor continued to increase, the landowners and the Jesuits continued to appeal to the government and the Crown on whether the Jesuits should have full claim on native slave labor. In 1574, Portugal decided natives who had already been converted and were living in aldeias were the property of the Jesuits. However, colonists initially used native slaves who had previously been enslaved through warfare with other natives. Of course, with such a great demand for slave labor, a slave trade quickly emerged, which was run by the slave capturers known as Bandeirantes.

Today, the Bandeirantes are likened to urban legends, similar to pirates. Although most imagery depicts the Bandeirantes as heroic Europeans, there were many more native Brazilians and *mamelucos* (people born from a native and European relationship) working as Bandeirantes. This is likely because much of the slave-capturing work required intense expeditions through the wilderness, which the natives were much more accustomed to. The Bandeirantes were almost entirely converted natives who probably used slave-hunting as a way to escape treacherous slave labor. Over the decades, the Bandeirantes began to diversify their work from mostly enslaving natives to acquiring land and searching for precious metals and minerals.

Despite allowing the non-missionaries to forcefully recruit their own slaves, the sugar plantations needed more labor than the Bandeirantes could supply. Similar to other colonies in the Americas, the Portuguese in Brazil began to import slaves from Africa to sustain their plantations and factories. Although the exact number of African slaves in Brazil is not known for sure, by 1600, there were thousands of African slaves in Brazil. The total number of slaves (both natives and Africans) more than doubled the population of the Portuguese settlers in most captaincies. The slave trade in Brazil predated that of the United States by nearly 150 years. It is estimated around 40 percent of the approximately ten million slaves brought to the Americas went to Brazil. By the time of the first official census, which would take place in 1872, Brazil's population was approximately 20 percent black, not including those who would come to be known as *pardos* (people of mixed-race).

Sousa's final instruction from King John III was to reinstate the monarchy's power in Brazil. Up until this point, the captaincies were running completely autonomously from the Crown. Settlers in Brazil had begun to feel independent from Portugal, and while they had brought their language, culture, and customs, the years spent living so far away in a territory so different from their homeland forced the settlers to develop new traditions and beliefs. As with most European colonies, as time passed, the Portuguese settlers in Brazil strayed from those still living in Portugal. There would be a rise in the requests for self-government and more independence from the monarchy.

Though settlers had only been living in Brazil for around half a century, by the time of Sousa's arrival, these wishes for autonomy had spread within the captaincies, especially the more successful ones. Although the *donatários* and settlers were not yet requesting total independence, these sentiments, which began as early as the

16th century, would fester over the years and lead to the revolution for independence in the 19th century.

Foreign Threats to Portugal's Claim on Brazil

Although the Treaty of Tordesillas ensured Portugal's ownership of Brazil in the eyes of Spain, the other European nations had not been involved in this agreement. As other countries began claiming land in the Americas for themselves, Portugal's claim over Brazil became threatened. In 1555, not long after Portugal established its first settlements in Brazil, France claimed the harbor of Rio de Janeiro, which had not been properly explored or developed by Portugal at this point.

The governor-general at the time, Mem de Sá, had to organize and lead a defense operation, which involved blocking the seaport entrances to Rio de Janeiro to surround the French settlers. The French troops surrendered soon after Mem de Sá's mission, and in the next decade, Portugal began making attempts to properly establish a settlement in the previously neglected Rio de Janeiro to prevent further attacks. The city of Rio de Janeiro was officially founded in 1567, twelve years after the French claimed the harbor.

Chapter 4 – The Iberian Union, Nieuw Holland, and the Portuguese Restoration War (1580–1668)

The Iberian Union

Although the Treaty of Tordesillas was rather vague and had been established before the European nations had a proper understanding of the layout of the Americas, for the most part, Spain and Portugal remained on good terms. That being said, there were some occasional arguments over territory, which resulted in small battles or readjustments to the boundaries of the Treaty of Tordesillas. While Portuguese and Spanish explorers were mostly on good terms, Portugal's relationship with Spain at home was quite different in the 16th century.

After the death of King John III in 1557, the Portuguese crown was passed to John's son, Sebastian, who was only three at the time. Thus, the kingdom was controlled by various regencies. Finally, in 1568, at fourteen years old, Sebastian took his rightful place on the throne, which he would hold for ten years. Considered to be a successful leader, despite his young age, Sebastian constantly strived to improve Portugal in more ways than most leaders.

Even at a young age, he dreamed of finding new trade routes to India. An opportunity presented itself when the sultan of Morocco arrived in Portugal, requesting help from Sebastian to clear Morocco of the Ottomans. When the sultan was reinstated as the leader, he offered Portugal safe passage through Morocco to India in exchange for military aid. Although King Sebastian was still young, unmarried, and childless, he decided to join his forces in Morocco in the Battle of Alcácer Quibir (Battle of the Three Kings). While his remains have never been found, it is assumed that King Sebastian died in the battle, along with the sultan of Morocco.

King Sebastian was succeeded by John III's brother, his great-uncle, Henry, who had previously served as one of his predecessor's regents. Henry was already sixty-six years old and a cardinal of the Catholic Church when he took the throne in 1578. Although he attempted to abdicate as cardinal so that he could marry and have a child who could serve as his heir, his request was denied by the pope, who did not want to get on the bad side of the king of Spain. The king of Spain at the time, Philip II, ensured Henry's request was denied, not because he was against cardinals being released from their religious requirements but because the lack of an heir would give him an opportunity to claim Portugal for Spain.

And that is exactly what happened when King Henry died two years after taking the throne. Although there was a race to claim Portugal, Philip II, who had been preparing for this opportunity, quickly stole the crown from other Portuguese competitors. It was agreed upon that if Philip II became king of Portugal, Portugal would be united with Spain, which meant Portugal and its colonies would not become provinces of Spain. This period of unification would be known as the Iberian Union, and it would last from 1580 to 1640.

Dutch Threats to Brazil

Philip II would remain the king of Portugal and Spain until his death in 1598. During his reign, Spain was experiencing its golden age, as it had profitable overseas territories and a strong military. Thus, Philip was able to ignore much of the bureaucratic and economic responsibilities as king and focus on pushing his strong Catholic views. Since King Philip did not invest in overseas resources or profitable foreign trading or improve his country's tax system, Spain's prosperity did not last long. King Philip and his successor, his son (who was also named Philip), would search for quick, new income sources.

King Philip II began taking advantage of the Netherlands, which was already unhappy with Spain, as it had helped to enforce a menacing Catholic presence during the Inquisition. King Philip II's decisions directly led to the Dutch War of Independence, which began in 1568 and continued for eighty years. Only twelve years after the start of the eighty-year war, Portugal was integrated with Spain, which meant Portugal and its overseas territories gained new enemies.

In May 1624, the Netherlands sent twenty-six ships with over three thousand men. They managed to successfully seize Salvador, the capital city of Brazil, as they caught the governor, Diogo de Mendonça, off-guard, forcing him to surrender. Salvador remained in the hands of the Netherlands for a little less than a year. In April 1625, the Portuguese finally outnumbered the Dutch troops, sending fifty-two ships and over twelve thousand men to Salvador. Although the face-off resulted in Salvador's return to the Portuguese, the Dutch returned to Brazil many more times in the future to seize what land they could during their war with Spain.

Dutch Seizure of Brazil and the Creation of Nieuw Holland

The second Dutch attempt at seizing Brazilian territory happened five years later. By the early 17th century, Brazil's, more specifically Pernambuco's, sugar industry was booming, and other nations had taken notice of Portugal's financial success. In 1629, the Dutch West India Company dispatched a fleet to Brazil, this time with sixty-seven ships, seven thousand men, and a better plan than their first attempt. The Dutch troops, led by Hendrick Corneliszoon Loncq, attacked Pernambuco on February 15th, 1630, and severely overwhelmed the Portuguese settlers and government. By February 17th, the Dutch troops had claimed not only Pernambuco but also Olinda, Recife, and the island of Antonio Vaz. Within a month, the Dutch set up a political council and began governing their Brazilian territories.

Over the subsequent years, the Portuguese staged revolts to attempt to win back Brazil. While there were minor victories, by the end of 1634, the Netherlands controlled most of the northern coastline of Brazil. Throughout 1635, Portuguese settlers escaped southward, away from the Dutch troops occupying Brazil, which was now known as Nieuw Holland.

Meanwhile, as the Portuguese were fleeing and plotting rebellions in the south, the Netherlands was reorganizing the north of Nieuw Holland and named Johan Maurits (John Maurice) as colonial governor. After arriving in Nieuw Holland at the beginning of 1637, Johan Maurits organized many conquests, specifically targeting Portugal's most profitable settlements in Nieuw Holland. Within one year, Johan Maurits led the Dutch troops in seizing Portuguese cities, plantations, and forts. By the end of his first year, the Netherlands controlled around half of Brazil, almost entirely in the north.

Maurits envisioned Nieuw Holland as a true colony of the Netherlands. Once most of the northern territory had been claimed, he began requesting money to develop the land. He sent invitations to Dutch artists, scientists, and political figures, hoping they'd see the potential that Nieuw Holland could offer the Netherlands. However, the Dutch West India Company, which was responsible for sending the first Dutch fleets to Brazil, was only interested in profit and saw no benefits in developing the land. Disappointed, Johan Maurits resigned as governor in 1644, and his successors mostly shared the Dutch West India Company's beliefs and goals.

Portugal's Dissatisfaction with Spain

Before Johan Maurits resigned as governor, Portugal was actively fighting a war of independence with Spain. In 1621, sixteen-year-old Philip IV ascended to the throne of the Iberian Union. Although his predecessors had stolen power from Portugal, King Philip IV would become known as the "Tyrant" and the "Oppressor." Almost immediately upon becoming king, Philip IV began unfairly raising the taxes on the Portuguese, specifically the merchants and elite. Although Portugal had agreed it would not become a Spanish province, Philip IV quickly began replacing Portuguese government positions with Spaniards and removed Portuguese nobles from the court.

While the Portuguese were not entirely satisfied with the way their country was being run by Spain, there had been few changes aside from their involvement in the war against the Dutch. However, King Philip IV went back on his predecessors' promises and attempted to strip the Portuguese nobles of their power and profits, which went too far. In 1634 and 1637, Portugal organized minor revolutions that resulted in very little. However, these insurrections proved the Portuguese were frustrated. Some kind of change would have to come.

The final straw occurred in 1640. Spain's prime minister at the time was Gaspar de Guzmán y Pimental, Count-Duke of Olivares, who had served as a personal attendant to King Philip IV while he was growing up and had remained utterly loyal to the king he had helped raise. Prime Minister Olivares's policies were mostly geared toward acquiring more power for the king. In 1640, this directly affected Portugal, as he tried to get the Portuguese military to battle the Catalans. The Catalans are an ethnic group mostly living in Catalonia in northwestern Spain who speak their own language, Catalan. Like the Portuguese, the Catalans were discontented with the Spanish Crown and had waged small revolutions to oppose Spain stripping the region of power and implementing changes.

Prime Minister Olivares was trying to gain control of the nation by using the military, but he miscalculated the implications this demand would have. Trying to force Portuguese troops to quell another dissatisfied region under the Spanish Crown was the last straw.

After sixty years of peace, a revolution was no longer a discussion. On December 1st, 1640, the revolution for the independence of Portugal, which was known as the Portuguese Restoration War, began. Catalonia would wage its own revolution at the same time, which came to be known as the Reapers' War.

Portuguese Revolutionary War

While all of Portugal was gearing up for revolution, three men would formulate the plot that freed Portugal from the Iberian Union. With the help of fellow dissatisfied Portuguese conspirators, Antão Vaz de Almada, Miguel de Almeida, and João Pinto Ribeiro took action by killing Spain's secretary of state, Miguel de Vasconcelos. They took the revolutionary action even further by taking King Philip IV's cousin, the duchess of Mantua, hostage.

While this plot was far more aggressive than Portugal's previous revolutionary attempts, the reason it was so successful is that it was perfectly timed to cripple Spain. In 1640, Spain was trying to fight intense revolutionary wars with Portugal and Catalonia and the Thirty Years' War, which had come closer to home and transformed into the Franco-Spanish War when France joined the fight. The imprisonment of a member of the Spanish monarchy helped to kick off rebellions in Portugal. Before long, most of the population began supporting the revolutionary battles in some form or another.

Soon, a new leader emerged for Portugal: John II, 8th Duke of Braganza, who was supposedly the grandson of Catarina, Duchess of Braganza. Due to Catarina's marriage into the aristocratic House of Braganza, she had been in the running to inherit the Portuguese throne before it was taken by Philip II back in 1580. According to the Portuguese and most historians, John became the leader the day (or soon after) the revolution began. However, John IV (as he would be known) was not technically sworn in as king of Portugal until the end of the Portuguese Restoration War in 1668.

The 1668 Treaty of Lisbon

In the years following the peak of the Portuguese Revolution, Portugal and Spain continued to war, and both countries rallied to find allies that could help them gain the upper hand. Under orders from the technically unofficial King John IV, during the 1640s and 1650s, representatives were sent to the courts of powerful western European countries. Portugal approached France first, as it seemed like a probable ally considering it, too, had been warring with Spain during the years of the Portuguese Restoration War. The Dutch, who still remained in control of Nieuw Holland (Brazil), were not interested in a treaty with Portugal either, and in 1641, they took control of Angola, another territory that belonged to Portugal.

Portugal finally found an ally in the United Kingdom, which was demonstrated in the marriage of King John IV's daughter, Catherine de Bragança, to King Charles II in 1662. Over the following years, the United Kingdom provided arms and soldiers to Portugal, which helped the Portuguese win crucial battles that would lead to the Treaty of Lisbon in 1668, ending the Portuguese Revolutionary War.

Brazil during the Portuguese Revolutionary War

While Portugal was distracted with its revolutionary war with Spain, the Dutch remained in control of Brazil, then known as Nieuw Holland. During these years, there were very few developments in Nieuw Holland because the Dutch West India Company saw no profits to be made in the territory. Despite its name, Nieuw Holland remained culturally and linguistically Portuguese.

That being said, Nieuw Holland was far from Portugal. After the colony was no longer under the control of Portugal, the inhabitants of Nieuw Holland began to forge their own distinctive culture, beliefs, and economy. Unlike in other colonies, intermarriage between indigenous people, African slaves, and Portuguese settlers helped to set apart the "Brazilians" from their European monarchies.

Although John Maurits remained as governor until 1644, the power in Nieuw Holland belonged to a few powerful families who controlled most of the territory, sugar mills, slaves, and farms. This is mostly because the Dutch population in Brazil remained very small. While there were a few thousand people who emigrated from the Netherlands and other European countries (other than Portugal) to live in Nieuw Holland, most of them were hopeful settlers, artisans, and merchants looking to create a new life abroad. Not wanting to invest too much money into what seemed to be an unprofitable territory, the Dutch West India Company sent very few politicians and soldiers to keep the population in check. Many members of the Dutch government in Nieuw Holland wrote to the Dutch West India Company, saying that the Brazilian population (made up of Portuguese settlers) always seemed prepared to launch revolts.

While the missionaries and Bandeirantes continued to explore the territory of Nieuw Holland, developments in the early to mid-17th century were really dependent on the elite. Few new cities were founded. Instead, powerful Brazilians built empires in the city surrounding their homes. The cities of Salvador, Rio de Janeiro, Recife, and Ouro Preto grew at unprecedented rates. Despite the fact some of these cities took many days to travel between, they developed culturally, economically, and socially in similar ways.

Brazil's Independence from the Dutch

After John Maurits resigned as governor, he was replaced by incapable Dutch leaders whose lack of authority strengthened the power of the wealthy Brazilian families. In the late 1640s, public dissatisfaction with the Dutch leadership continued to rise. While the rich Brazilian families, who were really just Portuguese settlers, helped to develop the economy and cities, the Dutch government reaped the benefits without putting in any work. Profits and products were being exported to the Dutch West India Company in the Netherlands, but little was being exported to Nieuw Holland in exchange.

The Dutch occupation upset the citizens since they still felt somewhat loyal to Portugal, but no one was more frustrated than the wealthy families, who were losing profits to the Dutch government. Although most of the Portuguese settlers were dissatisfied with the Dutch occupation, with many plantation owners and elites waging small rebellions, plantation owner João Fernandes Vieira is credited with putting the main rebellion into motion.

From 1645 to 1654, many battles were fought, most of which were won without any help from Portugal. Despite the shortage of food, the Brazilian-Portuguese settlers managed to defeat the Dutch in most battles. When Portuguese fleets arrived in Nieuw Holland with supplies of food, weapons, and men at the end of 1653, the Dutch had no choice but to surrender. A little over a month later, on January 26th, 1654, the Dutch signed a capitulation agreement, putting an end to their occupation.

Nieuw Holland returned to its original name, Brazil. For a few years, it continued to be developed and led by rich families without much aid from Portugal. Although the revolution freed the Brazilians from Dutch occupation and sparked sentiments of Brazilian independence, Brazil was not yet independent from Portugal.

Although the actual Dutch occupation in Brazil came to an end in 1654, the Netherlands and Portugal were still engaged in the Dutch-Portuguese War back home. Pretty soon after the capitulation agreement had been signed, a Dutch fleet caught Portugal by surprise and forced the Portuguese to agree to sign Brazil back to the Netherlands. However, after what had occurred in Brazil, the crippled Dutch West India Company was no longer interested in owning Nieuw Holland, and neither was the Dutch government, which at this time favored money over owning land.

Since Portugal wanted to govern Brazil and the Netherlands wanted money, writing a treaty was easy. On August 6th, 1661, the two countries signed the Second Treaty of The Hague. The treaty confirmed the sale of Brazil to Portugal in exchange for sixty-three tons of gold. Although Portugal would take approximately forty years to pay this debt to the Netherlands, the deal was certainly worthwhile, considering more than ten times their debt of gold would be discovered in Brazil in the coming gold rush.

Chapter 5 – Exploration and Brazil's Gold and Diamond Rush (1668–1800)

Exploration and Expansion in Brazil

Until the late 17th century, development in Brazil mostly clung to the coastline. Although some explorers and Bandeirantes found their way into the depths of the Brazilian jungles, the central territory remained mostly unexplored and completely uncolonized. This is partly because of the threats the terrain posed since it was difficult to navigate and filled with huge predators and unknown vegetation. The human inhabitants of the jungles were another reason the colonial explorers stayed on the coast.

In most colonies, the colonizers explored the territories of the indigenous population, often waging wars to claim the territory for themselves. This also occurred along the coast of Brazil, despite the fact the native people had lived there for thousands of years by that point. Though Portugal might have claimed the central territory of Brazil, a war in the unfamiliar dense Amazon jungle would not be one the colonizers could easily win. Hence, it was easier to simply allow the indigenous population to remain there.

Although missionaries attempted to set up schools and churches throughout the jungle, they realized it was easier to capture indigenous tribes and bring them to the missions they founded along the coast to convert them. Some brave cattlemen also attempted to traverse the inland of Brazil in search of land they could inexpensively acquire. However, they rarely ended up farther than a day's journey from the coast.

Other than that, the Portuguese settlers rarely ventured west or entered into the jungles until the Bandeirantes began their search for people they could capture as slaves. To put it simply, exploration and expansion were considerably slow in Brazil.

The Development of the City of São Paulo

In 1546, the city of Santos was founded. It was mostly located on an island along the Brazilian coast. As with most big colonial cities, Santos became a base for explorers, Jesuits, and settlers. Over the years, explorations branched farther out of Santos. In 1554, two Portuguese Jesuits founded a mission and a school about an hour outside of Santos in the township of São Paulo. Gradually, a community grew there that mostly attracted impoverished Portuguese farmers.

In the 16th and 17th centuries, to compete with the more affluent farmers in Brazil, it was necessary to have slaves. However, most people in the gradually growing São Paulo could not afford to import African slaves. Before long, the settlers found a solution to their labor shortage. They began organizing groups of raiders who would capture indigenous Brazilians to work on the settlers' farms as slaves. As previously mentioned above, these raiding groups became known as Bandeirantes, and they became the primary inhabitants of São Paulo.

Although the south-central territory of São Paulo would never quite break into the sugar industry as the northern coastal cities would, the partnership between the Bandeirantes and the farmers helped São Paulo's economy develop quickly. As the population of São Paulo grew and the farmers became richer, the demand for indigenous slaves grew, forcing the Bandeirantes to venture deeper and deeper into the jungle. While hunting for slaves, the Bandeirantes also hunted for gold or any precious stone or mineral.

The Portuguese originally acquired Brazil with the hope that it would be rich in metals, minerals, or stones, but nothing of value would be discovered in Brazil until the end of the 17th century. This is likely because most of Brazil's gold deposits were discovered quite a distance from the coast and were regions that had not yet been properly explored. That being said, according to records and orally transmitted accounts, a few courageous Bandeirantes did travel past the borders of modern-day Brazil into modern-day Colombia and Bolivia.

Unlike in other colonies, interracial marriages and children were extremely common in São Paulo, most likely because most early settlers were too poor to bring any women with them. Intermarriage occurred between the indigenous populations, the Portuguese settlers, and the African slaves, who were eventually brought to São Paulo once its inhabitants became wealthier. These relationships helped to quickly grow the population of São Paulo.

By the 17th century, São Paulo was a region of major economic and social importance in Brazil, and a majority of the workforce, other than the Bandeirantes and farm owners, were indigenous, black, or mixed-race. By the end of the 17th century, approximately 600,000 African slaves were transported to Brazil, which was more than anywhere else in North or South America at the time.

The Unification of Brazil

Despite Brazil's size, the settlers remained more integrated than in other colonies. Of course, the settlers brought the Portuguese language and their heritage with them, which differentiated them from the rest of South America, which was under Spanish control. Portuguese was taught to slaves and indigenous populations as well.

Although the various regions developed different economies, with the northeast focusing on the sugar industry and the south focusing on farming, similar patterns emerged. Powerful families controlled more the economy and the government. While trips were occasionally made between cities and regions of Brazil, most of the upper class and working class stayed in one place. The communities were linked by the immigration of Portuguese settlers and the Bandeirantes, the latter of whom traveled between the communities and into the jungles.

Over the course of the 17th century, tens of thousands of African slaves would be transported throughout Brazil. Their culture, customs, and traditions trickled into society, and while they were marginalized, their presence helped to unify the regions due to the settlers' commonly shared beliefs about having slaves.

Gradually, Brazilians began to diverge from Portugal as well. A big reason for this was intermarriage, which developed new identities, as the people no longer felt tied to the monarchy. Brazilian nationality would become extremely relevant with the discovery of gold.

The Discovery of Gold in Brazil

The Portuguese and Dutch began searching for gold in Brazil almost immediately upon settling it, but for decades, the settlers had little luck finding anything of value other than the pau do brasil (brazilwood). The early colonial economy was built off of agriculture, which was developed from seeds that came from Europe. Brazil provided available land and a decent climate but no actual products of its own.

By 1690, the Bandeirantes had traveled throughout much of the rugged mountains and jungles in the interior of Brazil, never giving up on the search for profitable resources. Although the exact date is debated, sometime around 1695, the Bandeirantes' endless search finally paid off when gold was discovered just north of São Paulo in the state presently known as Minas Gerais. More specifically, it is believed gold was first discovered in the city of Ouro Preto, which translates to "black gold." It is named after the black iron oxide that covered the gold found in the region. Ouro Preto was originally named Villa Rica, which translates to "Rich Village."

According to a paper written by Brazilian economists Joana Naritomi, Rodrigo R. Soares, and Juliano J. Assunção, the discovery of gold, as well as the sugar industry, still has noticeable negative social, political, and economic impacts on present-day Brazil. That being said, for better or worse, the gold rush had begun, and Brazil would never be the same.

Like other gold rushes, the discovery of gold in the Minas Gerais region caused the population of Brazil to change and grow at an exponential rate. Settlers living on the coast of Brazil made their way inland; for many, it was their first time venturing into the center of Brazil. The journey from Rio de Janeiro to Ouro Preto took nearly a week without horses. And since Brazil is huge, the trip could take several weeks, if not months, depending on the starting location. Thus, those living closest to Minas Gerais had the advantage of reaching the gold first, namely those living in Rio de Janeiro, Santos, and the region of São Paulo.

When the coastal populations finally reached Minas Gerais, they began setting up towns. The previously undeveloped inland of Brazil became quickly populated. Before long, word of gold made its way out of Brazil, and ships full of Portuguese immigrants began arriving in Brazil in search of their own fortune. There was such a boom in Portuguese immigration to Brazil that the Portuguese Crown attempted to enact strict restrictions and legislation to control the hordes of people attempting to settle in the colony. However, the immigration control policies were barely respected, and hordes of Portuguese settlers continued to arrive in Brazil.

At first, the gold rush was mostly a free-for-all. The gold was rather easy to find, and the area was completely untapped. However, within a few years, the rich gained advantages over the poor. Wealthier people were able to access better mining equipment and could employ slaves to speed up the discovery of gold. Thus, African slaves, some of whom had been transported specifically for the gold rush, helped to boost the population of Brazil.

In a letter written to the Portuguese Crown from the governor of Rio de Janeiro, gold was discovered "in such a fashion along the foot of a mountain range that the miners are led to believe that the gold in that region will last for a great length of time." Of course, gold gradually became less easy to acquire. Many of the wealthier miners experimented with methods to tap gold, which led to the development of various techniques, such as the use of troughs and hydraulic machines. Poor miners had to find their own methods of dealing with the gold scarcity. Many found themselves standing on the cliffs and banks above the creeks and using barriers or sluices, which would force intense gushes of water down below.

Before long, Ouro Preto became one of the most populous cities in the Americas, with an estimated forty thousand inhabitants by 1730. For comparison, New York City did not even have ten thousand people at this time. As the gold deposits in Ouro Preto became scarce, miners settled throughout the rest of the Minas Gerais region, exploring the new deposits that were constantly being discovered. According to records, approximately 400,000 Portuguese settled in Minas Gerais between the years 1693 and 1720. During the same time, it is estimated that around 500,000 slaves were transported to Minas Gerais as well. Although it is difficult to track down accurate population records from this time, historians believe that by 1725, Minas Gerais would have had around half of Brazil's population. In 1720, Ouro Preto (then still named Villa Rica) became the capital of Minas Gerais, and it would remain so until the end of the 19th century.

According to reports of the time, most of the immigrants who came to Brazil at this time were poor, as had been the original settlers in São Paulo and Minas Gerais. A Minas Gerais government official named José João Teixeira Coelho wrote of the people, saying, "They arrive here excited and with the hope of advancing their fortunes. The majority of them were either criminals or persons who at home had no more than what they earned with their hoe or by the offices they held. These men, who in Portugal were the scum of the masses and the despair of the elite, come to this enormous land of freedom to make themselves insolent and to play the role of nobles." This quote not only explains how impoverished the new Portuguese settlers were upon arrival but also the negative view the government had of the settlers.

As farmers began leaving behind their farms to mine gold, the larger population in Minas Gerais meant the demand and cost for food went up. Brazil suffered multiple famines, with two of the worst ones occurring in 1697 and 1701. Famine even struck in the north, which still had a steady revenue from the sugar industry since farmers and merchants refused to sell their products, instead traveling to Minas Gerais where demand was higher and products could yield more money. Although most of the miners were poor when they began mining, it is reported that a majority of the gold discovered in Brazil during this time was acquired by slaves.

In Minas Gerais, most of the gold would be found in riverbed soil, known as alluvial deposits, in numerous streams throughout the province. Unlike other deposits, gold found in alluvial deposits is relatively easy to mine. It does not require any major equipment, making it easy for small-scale miners to make major discoveries. All that was necessary for miners was a shovel, a gold pan, and a sluice box. A sluice box allows water to flow through it. The layers of filtered pans then catch various sizes of gold, minerals, rocks, or anything else found in the riverbeds. Of course, once most of the deposits were emptied, small-scale miners struggled. More complicated equipment was needed to dig below the alluvial deposits.

A miner using a sluice box.
No known restrictions; https://picryl.com/media/prospector-pouring-dirt-which-he-thinks-contains-gold-in-sluice-box-the-sluice

With such an influx of fortune seekers, it was inevitable that other gold discoveries would follow. And gold was indeed discovered in numerous other localities. Two new mining districts, Villa do Principe and Istabira, were proclaimed in 1715 and 1720, respectively.

Portugal's Impact on the Brazilian Gold Rush

Portugal very quickly tried to profit as much as possible from the discovery of gold in Brazil. The Crown attempted to sell small plots of land, but most of these deals did not go through. The Crown was so far from Brazil, so the territory quickly became something of a free-for-all. The gold rush moved too fast for the Portuguese Crown to keep up with selling land.

However, while the monarchy did not find profit in land sales, the gold itself was enough to satisfy Portugal, which had never given up on finding a profitable resource in Brazil. By the end of the 18th century, it is estimated that around eight hundred tons of Brazilian gold had been sent to Portugal. While some gold stayed in the colony, for the most part, the Portuguese Crown bought whatever gold was discovered in Brazil, although it did receive 20 percent of the gold for free and earned a lot of money off taxes.

The discovery of gold in central Brazil also led Portugal to finally focus on exploring away from the coast to search for other possible gold deposits or precious stones. Following the discovery of gold in Ouro Preto, other gold mines would be discovered in the Minas Gerais region and other inland territories. Gold would remain the most profitable Brazilian export for the first half of the 18th century.

The gold rush in Brazil was unprecedented. Although the limitations of the time meant the gold did not attract millions of hopeful immigrants to Brazil, it was the first major event that would shift the culture, population, and development of society. Since the Brazilian Gold Rush was the first of its time, the Portuguese Crown had no example of how to govern its colony through an event like this. It is reported that during the gold rush, the Crown became overbearing and attempted to govern and monitor everything, despite its distance from the colony.

In the rest of Brazil, Portugal had already relinquished most of its governing power to the local elite families. While all of the major cities still had governors and councilors, the economic and social development was truly in the hands of the rich settlers. However, in Minas Gerais, the Portuguese Crown succeeded in strictly governing the territory during the gold rush. Laws were enacted instructing all gold had to be brought to colonial mints, where they'd be pressed into bars or coins and exchanged for money. These mints were constructed all throughout Brazil, mainly in Rio de Janeiro, Bahia, and Ouro Preto.

Portugal established a 20 percent tax on all gold mined, documented, and sold to Portugal. This tax was common at the time; it was implemented in Spain as well, where it was known as *quinto real*, or the "king's fifth." Frustration with this tax led to lots of illegal gold sales. It is estimated that nearly half of the gold found in Brazil was exported illegally, either to family members back in Portugal or to other European countries that were offering a better price. Anyone who was caught distributing gold illegally to avoid the tax had their gold confiscated, with a third of the earnings going to whoever reported the crime and two-thirds going to the treasury. Portugal made more from confiscating illegal gold than it did from the "king's fifth" tax.

Taxes were also applied to other aspects of the gold rush, such as mining pans, slaves, and cattle entering or leaving Minas Gerais. In June 1720, the miners' dissatisfaction with the administration developed into a full-scale revolt in Ouro Preto, which was suppressed by Portuguese dragoons sent by the Crown to maintain order. After the failed revolution, the Crown enjoyed unchallenged control for many decades.

The Gold Rush Skirmishes

Throughout the gold rush, the large settlement of miners competing in the rivers for discoveries that could easily change the course of their lives quickly led to skirmishes. In 1706 and again in 1708, the skirmishes culminated in a small civil war that came to be known as the War of the Emboabas. The war was between the Paulistas, the original Portuguese settlers of São Paulo, and all of the new Portuguese settlers, who became known as the Emboabas. It is estimated that several hundred men were killed during the war, which led the settlers to seek help from the Portuguese Crown to create order. This demand for a government led to the establishment of a small administration in Minas Gerais.

Even with the presence of a governor, the war played out until the Emboabas won over the local Paulistas, forcing the Paulistas to share the gold deposits they had discovered. Throughout the early 18th century, the Paulistas, who had a better understanding of the region than the Emboabas, continued to discover gold mines farther west from Minas Gerais in Cuiabá, Goiás, and Mato Grosso. However, no matter how far westward they went, the gold deposits were always discovered by the Emboabas. Since, for the most part, the Paulistas no longer felt connected to the Portuguese Crown, the administration constantly sided with the Emboabas. In the years following the gold rush, the powerful Paulista families surrounding the gold mines lost their power to the Crown's administration.

How Portugal Used the Gold

Unlike the Portuguese monarchy, which mostly spoke of the prosperity and fortune that would come from the gold, the governor of Algarve, Portugal, Dom João de Lencastre, spoke of the threats the discovery of gold could pose for the monarchy. Governor Lencastre reportedly said the discovery of gold would not only hurt foreign relations but also be traded quickly for items of lesser value. This was not too far from the truth. Most of the gold Portugal acquired from Brazil was used to pay off debts to the Netherlands and Spain from the wars that had occurred before the gold rush. Gold was also used to construct incredible Baroque infrastructures, mostly churches, many of which can still be seen throughout Portugal.

In 1703, Portugal and England signed the Methuen Treaty, which enacted trading laws on Portuguese wine exported to England and English textiles imported to Portugal, which, at this time, were the main two products traded between the two nations. While this treaty was advantageous to England, whose textiles were greatly sought after at this time and easy to produce, it left Portugal indebted to England. This was mostly because Portugal could not maintain the wine supply needed to equate to the number of English textiles they imported. As predicted by Governor Lencastre, a good chunk of Portugal's gold profits went to paying back the deficit Portugal owed England.

Aside from paying off all of its debts, Portugal barely profited from the discovery of gold in Brazil. Unlike other monarchies that experienced "golden ages" when their colonies struck gold, the Methuen Treaty and overmining led to the depletion of gold before Portugal could really experience prosperity.

Brazil's Sugar Industry during the Gold Rush

Between 1650 and 1690, the years before the gold rush when Portugal had control of Brazil, sugar was Brazil's primary export. However, when gold was discovered in Minas Gerais, some of the most successful sugar plantation owners packed up and transported their slaves in hopes of striking it rich in the gold mines.

Since the demand for sugar remained the same and supply fell, the price of sugar more than tripled between the years 1634 and 1700. Inflation was also brought on by new slave taxes that were introduced due to the gold rush. Although sugar was being sold for far more, high labor costs meant plantation owners' profit margins dropped, leading even more sugar producers to close their plantations and head to the gold mines. Between 1650 and 1750, sugar went from accounting for 95 percent of Brazil's total exports to only 47 percent, while gold went from 5 to 47 percent.

The Discovery of Diamonds in Brazil

During the search for gold in Minas Gerais, miners continued to come across bright, transparent crystals that appeared to have no intrinsic value. Many of the men who caught these crystals in their gold pans threw them back, and some even used them for keeping score in card games. While it is difficult to confirm exactly how these crystals were identified, according to stories from around 1720, one miner showed his collection of crystals won in card games to a man who had traveled in India's Golconda region, which is rich in diamonds. Apparently, the man instantly recognized the worthless crystal for what it was: a diamond. Regardless of how the crystals were recognized as diamonds, by 1721, the diamond hunt was on.

By the end of the year, several diamond mines had been discovered. This was perfectly timed with the end of the gold rush and the diamond scarcity that had been happening in India, which had previously been the number one exporter of diamonds. Although Portugal had quickly monopolized the gold found in Brazil, it did not have a monopoly on Brazil's diamonds until 1739. While there is little historical documentation of what occurred, according to some Dutch historians, the Netherlands secured a monopoly on Brazilian diamonds through trades made years before. It is also possible the Dutch acquired a monopoly on the diamond trade after Dutch explorers were invited into Brazil to aid the Portuguese miners in securing the territory from the indigenous population.

According to accounts from Dutch explorer Jacob Roggeveen and his crew, "A little time before the arrival of Roggeveen [in November of 1721] the Portuguese had discovered a diamond mine not far from St Sebastian, of which at that time they were not in full possession, but were meditating an expedition against the Indians, in order to become sole masters of so valuable a prize; and with this view they invited the Dutch to join them, promising them a share in the riches in the event of success." Thanks to Brazil's diamonds, Amsterdam would become known as the City of Diamonds, as it was the home of the majority of the world's diamond polishing and trading at the time.

Although the Dutch profited greatly from the discovery of diamonds in Brazil, Portugal did not miss out on profiting from the diamond trade. Toward the end of the 1720s, when the discovery of Brazilian diamonds had finally spread throughout Europe, Portugal moved its focus from controlling the gold rush to the diamond rush. Diamond mining was restricted, and high taxes were introduced. As a result, illegal diamond smuggling quickly became commonplace. The most important result of the diamond rush for the Crown was not the profits earned but the status it gained. Brazil became one of the richest colonies in the world, and Portugal once again became a legitimate player in the European economic and political spheres.

Of course, not everyone profited from the discovery of diamonds in Brazil. Since diamonds became easier to discover than gold, African and indigenous slaves were quickly transported from gold mines to diamond deposits. The working conditions were similar, as the diamonds were mostly found in riverbeds in the Minas Gerais region. Water was redirected into sluice boxes that were panned by slaves under the watchful eyes of the European slave drivers.

The situation was also horrible for the indigenous population who lived in Brazil's interior. Gold and diamond mining meant European settlers were encroaching more and more on their land. Although there is little information in European history books about how the indigenous population was affected by the gold and diamond rushes, there are reports of small-scale skirmishes over land.

Interestingly enough, even three hundred years after the original discovery of diamonds and gold in Brazil, settlers are still warring with the indigenous population over the territory containing the precious minerals and metals. In an article written in 2015 in *Folha*, a Brazilian newspaper, the Cinta Larga tribe is still struggling to contain illegal mining in their territory, which is located in the western region of Brazil in Mato Grosso. The state prosecutor who is working to defend the Cinta Larga people, Reginaldo Trindade, is quoted as saying, "In March of this year, there were no less than 500 armed miners who told the Cinta-Larga that they would not leave the indigenous land."

Although it is hard to find reports of similar incidents from the 1700s, it is probable the situation was much worse and that a very large portion of the indigenous population from the diamond- and gold-rich regions would have lost their lives. The Europeans did not have much regard for the territory of the local indigenous population. Much of the mining was concentrated in the Jequitinhonha River, near present-day Diamantina, which was originally a village named Arraial do Tijuco.

Roads were quickly built throughout the Minas Gerais region, connecting the diamond deposits in Diamantina to the gold mines around Ouro Preto to the ports on Brazil's coasts. These roads became known as the Estrada Real, or the Royal Highway. They facilitated the transport of mined goods to Portugal. Since Rio de Janeiro held such importance as the primary port used for the export of diamonds and gold to Europe, it became the capital city of Brazil in 1763. Rio would also become the home to European settlers who moved to Brazil in waves in the second half of the 18th century.

The Jesuits in Brazil during the 18th Century

Since the original discovery of the colony, Portuguese Jesuits continued to focus on converting and recruiting labor from the local tribes. Throughout the early 1700s, the Jesuits were completely supported by the Crown, and unlike local farmers, the church did not have to pay any taxes on crops sold or slaves they employed. As taxes skyrocketed for the Portuguese settlers, who could not even transport cattle from one farm to another without paying a tax, animosity formed toward the Jesuits.

By 1750, the Portuguese Crown was no longer in favor of the Jesuits' complete autonomy in Brazil. When Sebastião José de Carvalho e Melo was appointed secretary of state, his main instructions from King Joseph I were to increase Portuguese profits and limit the church's power in Brazil. Gradually, the Brazilian Jesuits' autonomy was taken away. In 1759, Secretary Sebastião José officially expelled the Jesuits from Brazil, a move that was highly supported by the elite families.

Of course, not all of the Jesuits left Brazil. Many remained until 1773 when Pope Clement XIV officially mandated a crackdown on all schools, hospitals, and other church-run institutions.

Although the Jesuits could no longer enslave and convert the indigenous populations, conditions did not get much better for the local tribes, as the government began new initiatives focusing on "Europeanizing" the indigenous people. This "Europeanizing" was mostly accomplished through miscegenation, or forced interbreeding, between the European settlers and the indigenous population. Both the indigenous people and African slaves were constantly forced to betray their own just so they could survive in Brazil. White slaveowners forced their African slaves to beat one another. While there would be various slave revolts, Brazil continued to import millions of slaves until the mid-19th century.

Brazil at the End of the 18th Century

By the end of the 18th century, the people's desire for Brazil to become independent from the monarchy was at an all-time high. This was brought on by the high taxes and stricter laws. In 1789, José Joaquim da Silva Xavier, who would become known as the Tiradentes, or the "Tooth Puller" (he worked as a dentist), led the first Brazilian nationalist rebellion against the Portuguese monarchy. Although the Tiradentes's rebellion would fail, with José Joaquim da Silva Xavier being captured and executed, the Tooth Puller would go on to become a symbol of the nationalistic beliefs of the colony. A painting named *Tiradentes* depicts his execution. It was painted in 1893 by Brazilian painter Pedro Américo and shows that Tiradentes became a martyr for the Brazilian independence movement.

Overall, Portugal's decision not to develop an economy for the local Brazilian people, instead choosing to drain Brazil's resources, would cause a revolution for Brazil's independence in 1822.

Tiradentes by Pedro Américo.
https://commons.wikimedia.org/wiki/File:Tiradentes_quartered_(Tiradentes_escuartejado)_by_Pedro_Am%C3%A9rico_1893.jpg

Throughout the 1700s, as more information about Brazil spread throughout Europe, the colony became home to miners, artists, carpenters, architects, and merchants. Although slavery continued to be legal in Brazil until 1888, by the end of the 18th century, much of Brazil had been developed by African Brazilians (both slaves and free African Brazilians). Some of Brazil's most recognized artists and architects of this time were of African descent. The most notable were the sculptor and architect Antonio Francisco Lisboa (known as Aleijadinho) and the architect Mestre Valentim. Both of these men were half African and half Portuguese and had grown up in Brazil. Since they were born to white fathers, they were able to escape slavery.

Although censuses of the time are completely unreliable, they can help to shed some light on how the population of Brazil was living. At the end of the 18th century, a census from the time declared there were over three million people living in Brazil. In comparison, the approximate population of Canada was estimated to be two and a half million, and the United States at this time was over five million. Approximately 12.4 percent of the population of Brazil was free African Brazilians, while 49.4 percent of the population was slaves. Meaning that, at the time, over 60 percent of the population was assumed to be of African descent.

Although we can assume the census takers did not traverse deep into the jungle and all the way to the borders of the colony, it is estimated that at the end of the 18th century, there were 250,000 indigenous people in Brazil, which is around 7.5 percent of the population. This was a massive drop from the assumed millions of indigenous people who lived in Brazil before the arrival of the Europeans. Regardless of the effect on the indigenous people, with the help of the growing African, mixed-race, and Portuguese populations, the development of Brazil continued at exponential rates.

Chapter 6 – The Portuguese Court in Brazil, the Formation of Brazil's Monarchy, and Independence from Portugal (1800–1822)

The Napoleonic Wars in Europe

Although France had very little to do with the development of Brazil up until the 19th century, the Napoleonic Wars would have great effects on Portugal's richest colony. In November 1799, a coup d'état resulted in Napoleon Bonaparte becoming the leader of France. Napoleon's dictatorship began near the beginning of the War of the Second Coalition. Britain, Austria, and Russia wished to contain French expansion. Since Britain and Portugal had an alliance, Portugal joined the war.

By 1807, Napoleon had invaded most of Europe. That year, France allied with Russia, and the two powers attempted to take over the remaining countries, namely Great Britain and its allies, Portugal and Sweden. Since France was allied with Spain, access to Portugal was easy, and in July 1807, Napoleon demanded Portugal "close their ports to the British and declare war on Britain."

Portugal was also instructed to claim any British products in its ports and arrest any Englishman in the country.

Although Portugal was willing to close the ports and put an end to its relationship with Britain, the Portuguese Crown refused to arrest men and seize goods. This objection resulted in Napoleon ordering thirty thousand soldiers to invade Portugal. In October 1807, troops moved through Spain, arriving in Portugal on November 19th. Only ten days after the Spanish troops invaded Portugal, the Portuguese regent, Dom João, who would become known as King John VI when he actually ascended the throne, and the royal family fled to safety in Brazil.

This was absolutely unprecedented. Although royal families had visited their colonies before, Brazil would be the only colony in history to actually house the Crown. The Portuguese regent and his family finally arrived in Brazil in March 1808, along with numerous members of government and nobles escaping their war-torn home. The war, which mainly occurred between Spain and Portugal, became known as the Peninsular War and would last until 1814, during which time Portugal became the home of most of the warfare.

The Crown established a royal court in the capital city of Rio de Janeiro, which no doubt had a massive impact on Brazil's society.

The Royal Court in Brazil

Though many settlers shared the sentiment that Brazil should become independent from the monarchy, the arrival of the royal family was exciting for most. Until 1808, all royal orders had been sent from Portugal, which was, of course, far from the colony. The Crown had little understanding of what was actually happening in its colony. By the time updates were sent to Portugal and the royal orders reached Brazil, much had changed. Despite their nationalistic beliefs, it seemed many colonists believed the monarchy's arrival would be positive for Brazil, and Dom João and his family were welcomed with open arms.

Once stationed in Brazil, Dom João stopped seeing Brazil as simply a colony. João quickly terminated the strict commercial monopoly that Portugal had enforced on Brazil, opening the region up to legal trade with other countries. Brazil's port cities expanded rapidly, as merchants set up markets to take advantage of the abolition of Portugal's monopoly on Brazil's trade. Unsurprisingly, most foreign trade in Brazil would be conducted with Great Britain, which was Portugal's greatest ally at this time.

Dom João also rescinded a decree from 1785 that had been put in place to contain Brazilian manufacturing. For example, only cloth factories could produce sacks for food or clothes for slaves.

In 1810, the bond between Portugal and Great Britain would be furthered by the signing of the Strangford Treaty, which established a trade deal between Britain and Brazil. The treaty also decreed the British would be treated more fairly in Brazil than other settlers or visitors. British Protestants could continue to practice their religion in Brazil, despite the fact that Brazil and Portugal practiced Roman Catholicism.

Although the Strangford Treaty would put a strain on Brazilian agriculture and manufacturing, the trade agreement and allyship with Great Britain eventually helped Brazil grow its own economy.

Construction of Cultural and Government Infrastructures

While staying in Rio de Janeiro, Dom João gradually ordered the construction of more European establishments, such as a printing press, which opened in May 1808. In the late 18th century, the performing arts rapidly grew in Brazil, and the arrival of the Portuguese royal family only helped to expedite its growth. Although it is difficult to find much information on theaters or opera houses from the early 19th century, it is believed Dom João ordered the construction of a venue that could house performances. By the end of the 19th century, many iconic theaters had been constructed that are still standing in Brazil today.

Outside of culture, the royal family had a big impact on Brazil's military. Royal military academies were established, and military academies that had existed before the arrival of the royal court were updated. In the early 19th century, Brazil's armed forces grew exponentially. The Portuguese government utilized Brazil's army multiple times during its stay, including in the Portuguese conquest of French Guiana in 1809, in which Portuguese leaders and Brazilian troops, aided by Great Britain, successfully invaded French Guiana to weaken France during the Napoleonic Wars.

Since the government was operating out of Rio de Janeiro at this time, Dom João founded many government buildings in Brazil's capital city, including the Bank of Brazil and the Supreme Court. He would also establish a royal treasury, a royal mint, and a royal library.

The Monarchy's Return to Portugal

In 1815, Brazil, the Algarve, and the motherland of Portugal were reclassified as the United Kingdom of Portugal. This meant Brazil was no longer officially considered a colony. It would still be governed by the Portuguese Crown, though.

The following year, Dom João would officially become king of Portugal, becoming King John VI, when his mother, for whom he had been the regent, passed away.

While the situation was improving for most Brazilian citizens, the situation in Portugal had not improved much since the royal family had fled. Though the Napoleonic Wars would end in 1815 with the capitulation of Napoleon and the signing of the Treaty of Paris, the situation was never truly resolved between Portugal and Spain. Internally, European countries were suffering from the effects of the war, which led to various revolutions and civil wars.

As the small skirmishes finally culminated into large-scale revolts in Lisbon and Porto in 1820, King John VI of Portugal could no longer stay away.

The Establishment of a Monarchy in Brazil

When the Napoleonic Wars ended, King John VI of Portugal decided to stay in Brazil. This move disappointed loyal Portuguese citizens back home and angered other European countries, which saw this decision as foolish. In order to legitimize his decision to stay abroad, John VI decided to create the United Kingdom of Portugal. Until King John VI had to return to Portugal, Brazil functioned as an absolute monarchy, which completely changed the nation. Thus, when King John VI sailed home in April 1821, Brazil could not simply go back to being a colony.

Two days before he left for Portugal, King John VI named his son, Prince Pedro, as regent of Brazil, going against the wishes of the Portuguese Parliament, which believed Brazil should return to its colonial status once the royal family departed. While King John

VI was at sea, Parliament began attempting to reverse many of the changes that had reformed Brazil. For example, they wanted to terminate Brazil's free trade so that Portugal would once again have a monopoly on Brazil's products.

Dom (Prince) Pedro followed his father's example and stuck up for Brazil. After he refused to implement these changes, Parliament ordered him to return to Portugal. On January 9th, 1822, in response to the Portuguese Parliament's order to return home, Pedro proclaimed, "I shall stay." This iconic speech was named the "Fico," and his act of defiance is still celebrated as a Brazilian national holiday known as Dia do Fico.

That same month, Pedro formed a ministry and enlisted Brazil-born José Bonifácio de Andrada e Silva as his advisor. Like Prince Pedro, José Bonifácio was a strong believer in Brazil's liberation, and the two worked side by side to establish a central Brazilian government that could function without the help of the Portuguese administration. In June 1822, the two men established a legislative and constituent assembly, directly contradicting the interests of the Portuguese monarchy.

Though King John VI of Portugal, Pedro I's father, seemed to be a supporter of Brazilian liberation, he would not arrive home until July 1822. By this time, Portugal had greatly changed and was now being run by Parliament, which was not surprising since it had operated without the royal family for many years by that point.

Chapter 7 - Brazil's First Independent Empire under Pedro I (1822–1831)

Liberation of Brazil

After a few months of preparation, on September 7th, 1822, Pedro I declared Brazil's independence. Pedro was officially crowned emperor of Brazil on December 1st of that year, and his former advisor, José Bonifácio de Andrada e Silva, became Brazil's first prime minister.

Quoted in the book *A Documentary History of Brazil* by Bradford Burns, Father Belchior Pinheira de Oliveira, one of Pedro's confidants, said that on the day of Pedro's declaration, "Suddenly, he [Pedro I] halted in the middle of the road [while walking to their horses in the plains near the city of São Paulo] and said to me, 'Father Belchior, they asked for it and they will get it. The Côrtes is persecuting me and calling me an adolescent and a Brazilian. Well, now let them see their adolescent in action. From today on our relations with them are finished. I want nothing more from the Portuguese government, and I proclaim Brazil forevermore separated from Portugal.' With enthusiasm we immediately answered, 'Long live liberty! Long live an independent Brazil! Long live D. Pedro!' The Prince turned to his adjutant and said, 'Tell my guard that I have just declared the complete independence of Brazil. We are free from Portugal.'"

Of course, this simple statement to a few of Pedro's confidants would not be enough to convince Portugal and the world of Brazil's independence. Despite not having the approval of the Portuguese government, Brazil went on with ceremonies declaring its new independent status.

The coronation of Pedro I.
https://commons.wikimedia.org/wiki/File:Coroa%C3%A7ao_pedro_I_001.jpg

In the statement by Father Belchior Pinheira de Oliveira, Pedro was quoted as saying that he was viewed as an adolescent. He was known for being a bit of a player, as there were reports that he was having affairs with many wives of elite men. These affairs would be quite dramatic and often ended in the Portuguese government paying families to keep Pedro out of trouble.

However, by the time of Brazil's declaration of independence, Pedro had grown up quite a bit. In 1817, Pedro wed Maria Leopoldina of the House of Hapsburg, and together, they had seven children. Pedro would later have more kids with other women, so perhaps his "adolescent" phase never truly ended.

Why Was Pedro Coronated as an Emperor and Not a King?

It should be noted that Brazil specifically chose to coronate Pedro I as an emperor and not a king, as Pedro wished to make Brazil an empire rather than a kingdom. A king is a ruler who inherits his power through blood, which is exactly how Prince Pedro became king of Portugal after the death of his father, King John VI. Since Pedro was the son of the king of Portugal, he would technically earn his power from Portugal, which would make him beholden to the country.

Brazilians wanted to separate from the Portuguese monarchy, so Pedro I was coronated as an emperor. His power could be mandated by the people, and the ruler did not need to have a blood relation to the Crown. Essentially, the decision to coronate Pedro as emperor was a subtle yet powerful way of forging Brazil's own history and reiterated the fact it wanted no ties to the Portuguese monarchy.

Brazilian War of Independence

Interestingly enough, it is pretty difficult to find information about the first years of independence in Brazil. Most accounts seem to describe the transition as being rather smooth, which is likely because the other revolutions that were occurring at the same time in the Americas were violent affairs. Since Brazil did not go straight from the Portuguese monarchy to a parliamentary government like some former colonies, the transition was less difficult. Instead, Brazil went from being a colony to a dominion country to its own monarchy. So, when Brazil declared its independence from Portugal, Portugal was not suddenly losing a profitable colony since Brazil was no longer a colony.

However, Portugal was not happy with Brazil's decision to pull out of the United Kingdom of Portugal, especially because the courts were attempting to return the nation to its previous colonial status.

The Brazilian War of Independence began when Pedro first uttered his controversial "Fico" speech in January 1822. The Portuguese Crown decided that if Pedro would not agree to return to Portugal, then it would have to capture him and force him to come home.

In the same month as Pedro's "Fico" speech, Jorge de Avilez Zuzarte de Sousa Tavares, who was Brazil's military lieutenant general and a Portuguese royalist, dispatched the Brazilian military to capture Pedro. Pedro quickly prepared his own troops. Since most of Brazil was pro-liberation, it was not difficult for Brazil's future emperor to gather trained soldiers to prevent his capture.

The two forces finally met near Rio de Janeiro, but no actual fighting occurred. The standoff would not last long, as General Avilez's men withdrew to Portuguese fortifications.

For the next few weeks, Pedro and the liberation movement built their forces; however, they would never quite reach the strength of the Portuguese Legion. Although the Portuguese Legion was more powerful, General Avilez understood his attacks were limited. Attacking Pedro, who was not only the leader of Brazil but also the next in line for the throne of Portugal, would be dangerous and might lead to Avilez's death or loss of reputation. The Portuguese were also trapped in their fortifications and surrounded by Brazilians, who may not have been trained soldiers but were passionate about their cause.

After an intense battle, which resulted in the destruction of many of Portugal's original fortifications in Brazil, Avilez surrendered. For the next year or so, the skirmishes subsided in Brazil, but they would begin once again after Pedro I's coronation as emperor.

Again, there is very little information about what happened in the years following Pedro's declaration of independence, but most history books mention the first decade of independence was filled with many battles. Portugal would not recognize Brazil's independence until 1825, and there were still tens of thousands of royalists living in Brazil at the time, which means we can assume small-scale battles took place. Although thousands likely died during the Brazilian War of Independence, this was only a small drop in the estimated three million people who lived in Brazil at the time. In comparison to other wars of independence, the Brazilian War of Independence is not really a war at all but a series of small skirmishes.

Brazil's Economy after the Proclamation of Independence

Unlike other former colonies, whose economies often struggled after wars of independence, Brazil did not have to recover from a financially crippling war, and it had already been opened up to free trading. So, after the proclamation of independence, Brazil's national economy not only remained strong but would also grow exponentially. Brazil's sugar industry had been growing steadily since the 16th century, but only four decades after the proclamation of independence, the amount of sugar exported from Brazil nearly quadrupled.

After Brazil's independence, farmers also explored more agricultural venues. While many of these new products had slow beginnings, up-and-coming products followed similar patterns as the sugar industry. For example, cacao and rubber would really hit their peak in the 20th century.

The Tobacco Industry

One example of this exponential growth was in the tobacco industry. Tobacco had already been grown in the Americas before the arrival of the Europeans, and the indigenous populations were known to smoke tobacco far before it became mainstream in the rest of the world. In the 16th century, Portugal began cultivating tobacco in Brazil; however, it was mostly exported for use specifically by the royal family and the elites of society as medicine. When Portuguese farmers in Brazil began smoking tobacco for personal use, they realized the commercial potential it could have. Over the course of the 17th and 18th centuries, interest in and profits from tobacco grew substantially. At the end of the 18th century, the United States, Brazil, and Cuba were among the highest producers of tobacco.

After Brazil's proclamation of independence, it would rapidly establish factories that allowed for easier exportation, and gradually, its tobacco industry flourished. Today, Brazil is the second-highest producer of tobacco, with China being number one.

The Coffee Industry

Today, the number one export Brazil is known for is coffee. Coffee did not originally grow in Brazil, and its origins in the region are controversial. According to some accounts, the wife of a French Guianese governor helped a Portuguese lieutenant smuggle coffee seeds to Brazil after he seduced her.

Regardless of the actual origin, by the mid-18th century, coffee crops were common throughout Brazil. Until the 19th century, Brazilian coffee was mostly enjoyed by Portuguese settlers in Brazil; however, demand grew for the beans over the course of the 18th century. By the beginning of the 19th century, demand for coffee from Europe and the United States grew substantially, and by 1820, Brazil supplied nearly a third of the world's coffee.

According to some reports of the time, the amount of coffee exported from Brazil doubled from 1820 to 1860. As with the tobacco industry, this is partly because demand for the product skyrocketed. Brazil also doubled down on production, manufacturing, and exportation after it proclaimed independence. Around the 1860s, diseases spread in Asia that affected coffee crops, which gave South America's coffee industry another chance to boost profits. By the 20th century, Brazil would produce an estimated 80 percent of the world's coffee supply.

Emperor Pedro I's Rule

Although Emperor Pedro I claimed he no longer wanted to be viewed as an adolescent, many of the decisions he made were viewed as impulsive, authoritative, and somewhat immature. In 1823, Pedro I and Prime Minister José Bonifácio de Andrada e Silva had a difference of opinions, mostly because José Bonifácio thought the government should be more liberal and less authoritative. Angered by José Bonifácio's lack of support, Emperor Pedro I exiled his long-time advisor and his family and also dissolved the Constituent Assembly. The decision to dissolve the Constituent Assembly meant Brazil had to put a pause on attempting to write a new constitution that would help distinguish Brazil as its own nation separate from Portugal.

Although Emperor Pedro I would still be known as "the Liberator" of Brazil, public favor dropped after this controversial decision, especially in Brazil's northeast. The dissatisfaction culminated in the Confederation of the Equator, which was a separatist movement that sought to liberate Brazil from the new authoritative rule. As former Prime Minister José Bonifácio had predicted, Emperor Pedro I's strict authoritative beliefs were challenged and compared to that of Portugal's monarchy.

Brazil's Constitution of 1824

The general dissatisfaction with the emperor was not helped when Pedro I replaced the Constituent Assembly with the Council of State, which finished drafting the new constitution. The drafts were distributed to most of the administrative leaders, and they, for the most part, supported its immediate adoption. The new constitution would be instituted in 1824. The Brazilian Constitution of 1824 was rather liberal when compared to other constitutions of the time, although it still supported the centralization of government.

While Brazil would continue to be separated into provinces and municipalities with their own governments, the local administration's power paled in comparison to the central government, which was split into the legislative, executive, judicial, and moderating branches. The moderating power and the executive powers referred to Emperor Pedro I himself.

Legislative power was split into the Senate and the Chamber of Deputies, which together made up the General Assembly. The Senate positions were voted on by provincial electors but ultimately were decided by the emperor. Senators were instated for life. The number of deputies correlated with the size of the province. The number of deputies usually doubled the number of senators per province. Though the deputies were not chosen by the emperor (they were chosen by local electors), their terms only lasted four years, which meant they could not have the same impact as the senators, who were permanently elected.

The judiciary branch was made up of elected justices of the peace, judges who had life tenures and had to be trained in the law, a Supreme Tribunal of Justice, and provincial tribunals. While the judiciary system could operate without the emperor's direct involvement, Pedro I had the power to suspend or transfer judges, despite their life tenures.

The Brazilian Constitution of 1824 was overall rather progressive, which would result in it lasting for many years unchanged. That being said, the government and the emperor were strongly involved in the election process, which meant the central government was not truly liberally elected in any way. Since most municipal governments were made up of rich businessmen from the elite Portuguese families, who only focused on development when it advanced their personal finances, the centralization of government, which was necessary, was extremely controversial.

This was especially true in the north of Brazil, which was farther away from the capital. The people there felt distanced from Brazilian affairs and never really supported the coronation of the emperor. In the north, rebels began leading revolutionary movements that opposed the emperor and his new constitution.

The president of Pernambuco, Manoel de Carvalho Paes de Andrade, is likely one of the most notable rebel leaders of the time. He emerged as the leader of the rebellion known as the Confederation of the Equator.

As rebellions worsened in the northern provinces of Recife and Pernambuco, royal troops attacked the port cities, resulting in violent skirmishes. News of the attacks spread, and before long, so did the rebellions. In reaction to widespread revolts, violent civil wars between local governments and royal supporters began in Paraíba, Rio Grande do Norte, and Ceará.

Although dissatisfaction was strong in the north of Brazil, the emperor had a stronger support system. He had not only widespread Brazilian support but also the aid of the British military that was stationed in Brazil. The intense battles resulted in the execution of most of the rebel leaders. However, Paes de Andrade would manage to escape on a British ship heading back to Europe.

Finally, at the end of 1824, after almost a year of violence, royal commander Brigadier Francisco de Lima e Silva managed to establish order in the north of Brazil. All rebels, Andrade included when he returned to Brazil the following year, who wanted to remain free citizens of Brazil had to swear allegiance to Brazil's constitution.

The new constitution was accepted by Portuguese settlers in Brazil, especially in the more populated southern provinces. The 1824 Constitution abolished many of Portugal's strict legal punishments, establishing new laws and punishments that were distinctive to Brazil. The constitution also progressively protected the freedoms, laws, rights, and thoughts of Portuguese and European settlers. Although Catholicism remained Brazil's national religion and only Catholics could become deputies, the 1824 Constitution ensured religious tolerance for all Portuguese and European settlers.

Of course, it is necessary to highlight religious tolerance and the progressive protections of rights were only allowed to the Portuguese and other European settlers, as the 1824 Constitution continued to allow slavery of both Africans and the indigenous people. The new constitution did little to improve working or living conditions for the non-Europeans, as they would continue to suffer well into the 20th century, decades after the abolition of slavery which would come in 1888. The 1824 Constitution was representative of Brazil at this time. Brazil had an authoritative system that coexisted with a liberal charter of rights while coexisting with slavery.

Cisplatine Province of Brazil and the Creation of Uruguay

The Cisplatine Province was located in the very southern tip of Brazil.

A map of the Cisplatine Province.
Milenioscuro, CC BY-SA 4.0 <https://creativecommons.org/licenses/by-sa/4.0>, via Wikimedia Commons;
https://commons.wikimedia.org/wiki/File:Cisplatina_in_Brazil_(1822).svg

Since the Cisplatine Province was on the Portuguese and Spanish border, it was always contested, but ultimately, the region was determined to be the property of Spain in 1777.

Like other South American regions at the time, the Cisplatine Province, which was then known as the Banda Oriental, was frustrated with Spanish rule. In 1811, this dissatisfaction culminated in a revolution led by national hero José Gervasio Artigas. The rebellion would be successful in freeing the Banda Oriental, which would be renamed the Provincia Oriental in 1813. It was incorporated into the United Provinces of the Río de la Plata (or modern-day Argentina), and the population and administration grew rather quickly thereafter.

Artigas developed the republican Federal League of the Provincia Oriental, whose growing power and proximity to Brazil posed a threat to the emperor, who decided to invade in 1816. After three years of occupying the city of Montevideo and intense battles, Brazil's forces defeated Artigas's Federal League, claiming the Provincia Oriental for Brazil. It would be renamed Cisplatine and was annexed by Brazil in 1821.

Dissatisfied with Brazil's seizure of Cisplatine, the United Provinces of the Río de la Plata (Argentina) waged war with Brazil in 1825. Since the people of the region wanted independence, not to be annexed into either the United Provinces of the Río de la Plata or Brazil, the war was not very productive for either side.

After three years, in August 1828, the United Kingdom arranged a conference between the United Provinces of the Río de la Plata and Brazil, which gave Cisplatine its independence. The region was renamed the Oriental Republic of Uruguay.

Brazil's Growing Dissatisfaction with Emperor Pedro I

The Cisplatine War was not only extremely costly and time-consuming for the Brazilian monarchy but was also viewed as a huge mistake by the civilians of Brazil, who had little vested interest in the territory. After losing the war, the public's favor of Emperor Pedro I dropped significantly. Aside from the Cisplatine War, the emperor would find himself engaging in other controversies and was often at odds with the legislative powers of Brazil.

One of his controversial decisions included allowing mazombos to take positions of power in government. Mazombos were descendants of Portuguese settlers. However, with all of the intermarriages in Brazil, many of the mazombos were not completely Portuguese and may have had a non-white complexion.

Although many mazombos rose to hold positions of power and wealth in Brazil, many Portuguese settlers and both the Portuguese and Brazilian rulers would constantly view mazombos as second-class citizens.

Pedro I controversially allowed mazombos to take positions of power, a decision that was reinstated and revoked many times throughout Brazil's history.

The End of Pedro I's Reign in Brazil

In the years following the Cisplatine War for the liberation of Uruguay, Pedro I focused less on internal affairs in Brazil and even less on foreign affairs with other South American countries. Instead, Pedro I found himself forming relationships with European powers, mainly with Portugal and Britain. Some of the treaties Brazil signed during the final years of Pedro I's monarchy were seen as disadvantageous to Brazil, such as one with Great Britain that lowered the import taxes on Brazilian products.

As the people of Brazil lost interest in Pedro I, the emperor lost interest in governing Brazil and became increasingly involved in Portuguese affairs. Finally, in 1831, Emperor Pedro I decided to abdicate to take over the Portuguese throne, which had been waiting for him since his father's death in 1826. While Pedro would still be seen as the 'Liberator' of Brazil, he left the nation he liberated with a dissatisfied, unruly population and a struggling economy.

Chapter 8 – Brazil's Regency Period, the Empire of Pedro II, and the Collapse of Brazil's Monarchy (1831–1889)

Emperor Pedro I's Successors

On April 7th, 1831, Pedro I officially abdicated, leaving the empire to his five-year-old son, Dom Pedro de Alcântara. Although the young Pedro was Pedro I's seventh child, he was the oldest still living male descendent of the first emperor of Brazil. Pedro I's firstborn daughter, Maria, was already living in Portugal at the time of her father's abdication. When King John VI passed away, Pedro I was still the ruler of Brazil, and the next reliable heir to the throne was Maria, who was only seven years old at the time.

After King John VI's death, Portugal was led by a regent. However, the nation was building toward a civil war and needed a true, fair leader. In 1831, Pedro I abdicated, taking over the Portuguese throne from his unpopular brother, Miguel I, who had been acting as regent. Pedro I died in 1834 in Portugal, and after his death, his fifteen-year-old daughter Maria took the throne.

Brazil after Pedro I's Abdication

Similar to what had occurred in Portugal before Pedro I's arrival, Pedro II was only five years old at the time of his father's abdication, which meant the Brazilian monarchy had to be led by a regent until Pedro II was old enough to take the throne.

In this iconic painting titled, Acclamation of Pedro II on 9 April 1831, painted by Jean-Baptiste Debret, you can see crowds of government officials and soldiers crowding around Brazil's Imperial Palace, where young Pedro was standing, waving out the window at his future empire.

https://commons.wikimedia.org/wiki/File:Aclama%C3%A7%C3%A3o_de_D_Pedro_II_e m_1831_by_Debret.jpg

Between 1831 and 1840, Pedro II was tutored in not only typical school subjects of the time but also in politics so he would be prepared to lead Brazil, hopefully by the age of eighteen. One of his teachers was ex-Prime Minister José Bonifácio de Andrada e Silva, who had returned to Brazil in 1829 after being exiled.

The day after Pedro I's abdication, the National Assembly, looking for a way to calm down and unite the people of Brazil, put out a proclamation. We have included it here as translated and quoted in Bradford Burns, *A Documentary History of Brazil*.

The National Assembly's Proclamation of 1831

"Brazilians! Your conduct has been above all praise; that detestable faction, which dared to insult us in our homes, has witnessed another proof of our greatness, in the moderation which we have observed after our victory.

"Adopted Brazilians, who have been urged to strife by perfidious suggestions, be assured that it was not a thirst for vengeance, but the love of liberty, which armed us; and that the security of your persons and property will all be respected, whilst you obey the Laws of the magnanimous Nation to which you belong.

"The Brazilians hate tyranny, they abhor the idea of a Foreign yoke, but it is not their intention to hold a rod of iron over the conquered, or to avail themselves of their triumph in order to gratify rancorous passions?

"Fellow citizens, we have a Country, we have a Monarch, the symbol of your union, and of the integrity of the Empire; who, being educated in the midst of us, will receive almost in the cradle the first lessons of American liberty, and will learn to love that Brazil which witnessed his birth: the woeful prospect of anarchy, and of the dissolution of the Provinces, which was presented to our view, disappeared as it were in an instant, and was substituted by a more cheerful scene.

"All, all is due to your resolution and patriotism, and to the courage of the Brazilian Army, which put an end to the wild dreams of tyranny."

This proclamation is extremely revealing and helps us understand the mindset of Brazilians in the 19th century. In the second paragraph, the National Assembly reaches out to "adopted Brazilians" or settlers who likely are of Portuguese or European descent and may have seen the Brazilian revolutions as unnecessary. The assembly explains that these wars were not unreasonable because Brazilians "hate tyranny" and that it was the "love of liberty" that armed the people. This message addresses not only the nationalistic sentiments of the Brazilian people but also the concerns new settlers might have had.

After the northern provinces of Brazil rebelled, the National Assembly tried to contain the nation as it transitioned into the hands of inexperienced regent leaders, and the easiest way to do so was to give them the idea of liberty to look forward to.

Brazil's Provisional Triune Regency 1831-1835

In the first years following Pedro I's abdication, the administrative leaders of Brazil decided it was necessary to elect multiple regents rather than just one to keep the peace in the very divided nation. The triple regency was made up of three men: Francisco de Lima e Silva, Nicolau Pereira de Campos Vergueiro, and José Joaquim Carneiro de Campos.

Royal commander Francisco de Lima e Silva, who was the military leader who helped end the revolutions in the northern provinces of Brazil during the Confederation of the Equator, represented the royalists and the new Portuguese settlers. Vergueiro was a politician and businessman who helped write the 1824 Constitution and appealed to the liberal population of Brazil. He was also known to advocate strongly for the abolition of slavery. José Joaquim Carneiro de Campos was a politician who had been in the original Constituent Assembly and is credited with helping to draft a good portion of the 1824 Constitution. After Pedro I dissolved the Constituent Assembly, Campos left the government because he was dissatisfied. He somewhat represented the nationalistic northern Brazilians or as close as Brazil was willing to get without actually electing an anarchist nationalist to be a regent. Campos would eventually be replaced by João Bráulio Muniz from Brazil's northeastern state of Maranhão.

This temporary regency was known as the Provisional Triune Regency, with triune meaning "to consist of three." Although the Brazilian administration had good intentions when electing the three men to form the provisional regency, the next few years would be some of Brazil's least stable to date.

During the regency period, which would continue until 1840, rebellions in Brazil would not only continue but also spread from northern Brazil to the rest of the nation. For example, in the first two years of the regency, Rio de Janeiro alone had five separate uprisings. However, unlike the rebellions in the north, which were mostly centered around liberation, uprisings occurred for a variety of reasons. The liberation of Brazil was, of course, still being fought for, but there were also many revolutions for human rights and the abolition of slavery. The fight against slavery was especially widespread at the time since the contraband slave trade became extremely prevalent in Brazil in the 1830s. The slave trade in Brazil ended in 1831, but that didn't stop people from trying to get more slaves from Africa.

One of the main issues Brazil faced at the time involved the government. The government was very centralized, yet the provinces were widespread, and the economy varied so much in each province. Similar to what was occurring in the United States and other massive territories, areas that relied on farming and the exportation of agricultural goods relied on slavery. Provinces that relied more on manufacturing supported immigration. Regions that could survive without exports could afford to support the abolition of slavery and be against immigration.

Throughout the four difficult years of the Triune Regency, it became increasingly obvious the current system was not working. The three regents struggled to work together, and the people did not support all the power being in the hands of the centralized government. The provinces differed too much to be under one administration.

By 1834, Brazil was in a serious financial crisis, despite having so many profitable resources. One of the reasons for the economic struggle was that much money was being dispensed into the rebellions. The government had to repair damages and finance and train the military. Little change was being made, yet the early 1830s were essentially a series of never-ending uprisings, leaving everyone frustrated.

Another important event that affected Brazil at this time was the death of the first emperor, Pedro I. Despite leaving behind a frustrated nation and having abdicated to become king of Portugal three years prior, Pedro I's death in 1834 shook the nation. Brazil likely did not separate at this time because it had a very strong imperial military to suppress the uprisings. Additionally, many of the revolutions focused on the abolition of slavery instead of separating from the nation. Brazilians also wanted to become a nation-state; they wanted to be liberated but not separated from one another.

The Acto Adicional of 1834

Within a few years, it became obvious the current regency system was not working, which is why an amendment known as the Acto Adicional of 1834 was made to the Brazilian Constitution. This amendment was specifically meant to appease the revolutionary nationalistic republicans of Brazil, who were frustrated with the centralization of power and felt that Brazil's 1824 Constitution was authoritarian. This amendment notably gave more power to local leaders by allowing the creation of provincial assemblies, which helped to slightly decentralize the government. The provinces were now in control of education, at least at the primary and secondary school levels.

The provinces could also terminate the entailing of estates, which had previously allowed families to keep properties in the family for centuries, even though the original division of land was no longer practical for the growing cities. This meant the provinces could rezone and redivide the land.

The Acto Adicional of 1834 also replaced the Triune Regency with a single regent, Diogo Antônio Feijó, who would only be allowed a maximum four-year term.

Diogo Antônio Feijó's Regency, 1835-1837

Diogo Antônio Feijó had many jobs before he was the regent of Brazil. He was a priest, professor, provincial court deputy, and Secretary of State for Justice Affairs. During his time as a court deputy, he was known to speak openly about the threat Portuguese administrators posed to Brazilian rights.

Despite his past defense of Brazilian liberties, Feijó struggled to suppress the revolutionary uprisings that continued during his regency. This was obvious during the Ragamuffin War, which lasted from 1835 to 1845. One of the main reasons behind the Ragamuffin War was the lack of provincial power and the differences in economies around Brazil, which led Rio Grande do Sul to seek separation from the nation.

Another example of a smaller-scale uprising is the Malê Revolt of 1835, which was a slave rebellion led by Muslim African slaves living in Brazil. Although it only lasted one day, the Malê Revolt was so violent that it made worldwide news and led to the creation of the

Brazilian National Guard. Historians also credit the Malê Revolt as helping to speed up the abolition of slavery in Brazil.

Only two years after taking the position, Feijó forcibly resigned. Despite openly supporting the abolition of slavery, the ex-regent would end up owning a sugar mill with at least ten slaves before reentering politics years later.

Pedro de Araújo Lima's Regency, 1837-1840

In 1837, Feijó's successor, Pedro de Araújo Lima, became regent of Brazil after a lengthy career in Brazilian politics. Like Feijó, the new regent struggled to contain the Brazilians' frustration with the central government, and the revolutions that had been occurring since the start of the 19th century continued through his regency.

Some of the more notable rebellions took place in Salvador (known as the Sabinada, taking place from 1837 to 1838) and in Maranhão (known as the Balaiada rebellion, lasting from 1838 to 1841). The revolutions highlighted the same issues as before, such as the provinces' financial struggles, the centralization of the government, the slave trade, and the division of land.

Despite the fact that every province in Brazil followed similar development patterns in the 17th century since they were mainly centered around the sugar and agricultural industries, by the 19th century, they each had, and still have, a unique economy, culture, population, and political divisions. Grouping them all into one country, one government, and even one book is extremely difficult. However, regardless of the differences between all the provinces, almost everyone could agree on one thing: the regency system was not working.

The Crowning of Emperor Pedro II, 1841

Despite initially wanting to wait until Pedro II was eighteen to officially take his place on the Brazilian throne, Brazil's growing frustrations with the regents forced Parliament to reconsider their original plans. The members of Parliament decided that even though the people of Brazil did not want a central government, they would be far more likely to support the young, inexperienced Pedro II, son of the "Liberator of Brazil," than an unfamiliar, government-elected regent. On July 18th, 1841, at only fifteen years old, Pedro II was crowned emperor of Brazil, officially putting an end to Brazil's regency period.

According to Pedro II's confidants, the young emperor would have preferred to have been a teacher. Despite being forced into a position he didn't want to take at such a young age, Pedro II was known to be kind, fair, and curious. He reigned with the qualities of a gentle, understanding schoolteacher, which were revealed in his nickname, the "Magnanimous," meaning generous, forgiving, and noble.

Even though the regency period had left Brazil unstable and at war, Parliament was correct in thinking the Brazilian people would rally behind the young emperor. Pedro II ruled for nearly six decades, and although his reign ended in disaster, his time as emperor is considered by many historians to be Brazil's most fruitful period. The empire was run not only by the emperor but also by the continued support of the parliamentary government and the minister of war, Luís Alves de Lima e Silva, who was the son of one of Brazil's first regents, General Francisco de Lima e Silva.

Although Parliament was still split into the executive, legislative, judicial, and moderating powers, it acted as one power. According to historian Richard Graham, "No particular political philosophy distinguished one group from another." Of course, it must be noted that despite not officially being a part of the central government, the rich landowners, who became known as the "lords of the land" (*senhores da terra*), also played a massive part in the politics of Brazil.

Although the dissatisfaction with having a centralized government continued, Pedro II was certainly a more popular leader than his predecessors. During his reign, he managed to maintain peace in a divided nation. Brazil's prosperity at the time is documented in the travelogue titled "Brazil; its provinces and chief cities; the manners & customs of the people; agricultural, commercial, and others statistics taken from the latest official documents" published in 1866 by an Englishman named William Scully who was traveling in Brazil. In the words of Scully:

"The laws of Brazil are far from perfection, but its constitution is upheld in its integrity, and gives a sufficient guarantee to every one of life and property. Foreigners are welcomed, and the people and

Government endeavor by every means to encourage emigration; and, with the great facilities afforded, and the immense field for enterprise for industrious agriculturists, it is surprising that Scotch and Irish emigrants do not seek this country, where a life of more prosperity and of greater ease awaits them than can be realized in the United States, where the foreigner is despised, and where the frightful winter of an arctic clime exacts from the panting farmer excessive labour in a summer heat that is never experienced even in the hottest equatorial regions of Brazil.

"It is not too much to say that it is to the wise and vigorous administration of the present Emperor that Brazil owes her present rank among civilized nations, and the prosperity and tranquility she has enjoyed for so many years in the midst of the continuous outbreaks against law and order which have desolated and ruined the unhappy republics that surround her."

In Scully's quote, he mentions that Brazil is comparable to other civilized nations, such as the United States, because it has not had to live through the continuous wars and uprisings that have devastated the other nearby republics.

Despite the never-ending revolutions that continued throughout the 1820s to the 1840s, the uprisings were never as destructive as in other South American countries. Many historians theorize this was because of Brazil's gradual transition to independence. Unlike other nearby Latin American countries, which had to fight intense wars for freedom, Brazil was able to stop being a colony peacefully since Emperor Pedro I was pro-liberation.

Brazil's Military and Foreign Affairs during Pedro II's Reign

Although there still was frustration among the Brazilian people, by the 1850s, Brazil was peaceful, which gave Pedro II the opportunity to get involved in external wars and foreign affairs. Like his father, who got a little too involved with Brazil's neighbor to the south during the Cisplatine War, Pedro II focused a lot of his energy on affairs in Uruguay and Argentina.

In the early 1850s, the Brazilian Army helped Argentina overthrow its dictator, Juan Manuel de Rosas, in the Platine War. In the 1860s, Pedro II would similarly involve himself and the Brazilian Army in the civil war in Uruguay.

Brazil became somewhat of a superpower in the Americas; at this time, only the United States had a similar economy, power, and foreign relations. It would take decades for other American countries, such as Canada, to catch up to Brazil and the USA. This power left many surrounding countries feeling threatened by Brazil, which was demonstrated when Francisco Solano López, dictator of Paraguay, declared war on Brazil. This war would first be known as the Paraguayan War, but it would become known as the War of the Triple Alliance when López went after Brazil's new ally, Argentina, with Uruguay coming to support Brazil and Argentina.

War of the Triple Alliance, 1864-1870

As noted by William Scully, South America in the 19th century (other than Brazil) was going through some horrendously destructive wars, yet none are considered to be more devastating than the War of the Triple Alliance, which was the only major war that directly involved Brazil.

After years of intense border and tax disputes between Brazil and Argentina and their less powerful neighbors, Paraguay and Uruguay, dictators swept in, promising to help the struggling countries reach their full potential. Although Brazil helped fight off the Uruguayan dictator, transforming the nation into an ally, Paraguay waged war on Brazil before Pedro II had the opportunity to prevent it. Unlike Uruguay, the Paraguayan people seemed to mostly support Francisco Solano López, which made Paraguay's forces that much stronger.

Brazil, Argentina, and Uruguay officially allied together and declared war on Paraguay in May 1865. Although Brazil had been building up its army and, combined with Argentina and Uruguay, had a stronger army than Paraguay, Paraguay had been preparing for the war and had already built up an army of around fifty thousand trained soldiers.

Paraguay began the war on the offensive and invaded the southern territory of Rio Grande do Sul in Brazil. The allies managed to force the Paraguayan army to retreat from Brazil, and after a nearly two-year campaign, the Paraguayan forces had been forced back into Paraguay, with extreme costs to both sides.

In January 1868, Luís Alves de Lima e Silva took control of the allied army, and only a month later, he led an offensive military campaign into Paraguay with Brazilian armored vessels. Intense, violent battles continued in Paraguay for the following two years until 1870, when Paraguayan dictator, Francisco Solano López, was killed in battle, putting an end to the destructive War of the Triple Alliance.

Although all of the countries involved would be deeply affected by the war for years to come, no nation would suffer more than Paraguay, which had been host to most of the warring over the years. Due to a combination of bloody battles, malnutrition, diseases, and the cruelty of its dictator, Paraguay lost more than 300,000 people, leaving the nation with just a little more than 200,000 people. It is estimated that only twenty-eight thousand of the remaining population were men.

Both Argentina and Brazil would claim previous Paraguayan land as their own. Brazil added the annexed territory to grow its province of Mato Grosso. The intense five-year War of the Triple Alliance also had some profound effects on Brazil, other than just the annexation of territory. The war allowed Brazil to get closer to the abolition of slavery since hunting down escaped slaves had previously been the military's or government's job. During the war, they were primarily focused on the war efforts, leading to the liberation of many Brazilian slaves.

Also, like the Cisplatine War, the War of the Triple Alliance put a huge strain on Brazil's economy. Even though Pedro II helped Brazil's economy to flourish after the financial crisis it suffered during the regency, many young Brazilians questioned how much the emperor was helping the empire. This opinion became especially prevalent after the War of the Triple Alliance, as many young Brazilians became officers and were inspired by the Brazilian Marquês (Marquis) de Caxias Luís Alves de Lima e Silva. Many historians credit the end of the monarchy to the War of the Triple Alliance.

Brazil's Economy in the 19th Century

Despite the fact that it took centuries for Europeans to discover any profitable resources in Brazil, Brazil's economy was reliant on a few agricultural products or raw resources. The small brazilwood exportation came first, followed by the creation of the sugar industry, the gold rush, and tobacco farming. In the 19th century, coffee dominated Brazil's economy.

As with the other agricultural industries, the coffee industry was run by Brazilian settlers who were mostly of Portuguese heritage. They used slaves to keep up with the incessant demand for their products. However, unlike the sugar industry and the other previous agricultural ventures, Brazil's coffee industry came at a more modern time. Since society was rapidly advancing, with the people demanding change, coffee had a deep impact on Brazil's economy and infrastructure.

Although Brazil's raw resources had been exported globally for nearly a century, the coffee industry would truly help to put Brazil on the international playing field. By the end of the 19th century, coffee would take over even the sugar and mineral industries. Coffee became so synonymous with Brazilian culture that coffee plants made their way onto the Brazilian coat of arms, which was redesigned in 1800. Coffee would go from being basically a non-existent export in 1800 to accounting for nearly half the exports in the 1840s to being the majority of the exports in the 1890s.

While the rise of coffee as the next cash crop did not completely reverse the cycle of the colonial, feudal, extraction economy, it did encourage industrialization, help to develop a middle class in the country, and devalue the institution of slavery.

Brazil's Slave Trade and the Abolition of Slavery

Until the end of the 19th century, the coffee industry would be mostly based north and west of Rio de Janeiro, specifically in the Paraíba Valley. Eventually, with the overcultivation of land and the rapid increase in demand, the coffee plantations would move farther southwest into São Paulo.

Like the other agricultural industries in Brazil, the elite landowners who dominated the coffee industry played a large, controlling role socially and politically. To be able to keep up with demand and limit competition, coffee plantation owners had massive farms with hundreds, if not thousands, of slaves.

However, by the mid-1800s, Brazil's views on slavery had greatly changed, and there were fewer slaves living in Brazil than freedmen and descendants of slaves. With the pressure mounting both internally and externally to abolish slavery, Pedro II promised to gradually put an end to slavery in Brazil. Of course, this would not be an easy task, considering the massive role the Brazilian elites played in the nation-state's economy, politics, and society.

Both the emperor and Parliament decided the only way to abolish slavery without creating complete anarchy would be to phase in the abolition laws gradually. Small decrees were made, making it extremely difficult to trade slaves, especially transatlantically. However, much would stay the same until the 1870s, despite the growing demand for the abolition of slavery during the 1860s.

During the 1860s, massive anti-slavery rebellions were occurring monthly throughout the nation. The rebellions for the abolition of slavery became especially prevalent when nearby nations began abolishing slavery, such as Argentina in 1853 and the United States in 1865. Britain, which had remained an important trade partner with Brazil, was also pressuring its ally to hurry up and abolish slavery.

In 1871, Pedro II finally passed an anti-slavery law called the Law of the Free Womb that would make a real difference. As the name indicates, this law ensured the freedom of children born in Brazil, even if they were the children of slaves. While this was a step forward, it did little to help those who were still enslaved in Brazil, and before the year was over, abolitionists were already demanding more.

By the 1880s, no real advances in the abolition of slavery had been made. Although a majority of the population were abolitionists at this point, they were spread out throughout the nation. The pro-slavery Brazilians still held power. Lawyer Joaquim Nabuco de Araújo became the leader of the abolitionist movement, which was not surprising, considering he was the son of Brazilian Senator Jose Thomas Nabuco, who had openly supported the abolition of slavery. The younger Nabuco went as far as to write an entire book on the necessity of abolishing slavery called *Abolicionismo* (*Abolitionism*, written in 1883), in which he writes, "slavery was poisoning the very life of the nation."

During this time, there was a lot of concern from not only Brazilian elites but also Europeans and Americans that Brazil could never truly become a "modernized, civilized country." Some argued it was the climate (many Europeans believed that civilized people lived in colder climates), while others claimed Brazil's mixed "non-pure white" race would hold it back. One of the reasons Brazilian elites were so unsupportive of the abolition of slavery was that they feared Brazil, a country so dependent on agriculture, could not continue to keep up with leading countries without slaves. This was such a legitimate concern in the mid-19th century that Nabuco even addressed it in his book:

"If a nation can progress only by using the forced labor of an extra-legal caste, then it is a mere first approximation of an independent and autonomous state. If a race is able to develop in a latitude only by making another race work to support it, then that race has not yet attempted to acclimatize. Traditional Brazilians think that a Brazil without slaves would quickly perish. Even that result would be better than a life that can be maintained only by undermining national character and humiliating the country ... It [ending slavery] would summon forth new qualities in our national character and launch the nation on an epoch of progress and free labor, which would be the true period of our definitive development and our real independence."

Nabuco's movement and arguments, which were backed by millions of abolitionists living in Brazil, were extremely successful. Before long, state governments began abolishing slavery. In 1884, the states of Ceará and Amazonas set a precedent by abolishing slavery, which led many landowners in other states to free their slaves. In 1885, the national government, which was still lagging behind other neighboring countries, established the Sexagenarian Law, which liberated slaves over sixty.

In 1887, sixty-two-year-old Pedro II fell quite ill. The stress of holding together a divided nation couldn't have helped, and he went to Europe to seek treatment. While he was gone, his daughter, Princess Isabel, acted as regent, which she had done before when the emperor traveled. Due to her gender and the royal family's declining power, many questioned the legitimacy of Princess Isabel's regency.

However, after nearly a year as regent, in which time she replaced Brazil's parliamentary cabinet, Isabel passed one of the most revolutionary decrees in Brazil's history. On May 13th, 1888,

Princess Isabel declared the complete abolition of slavery in Brazil, freeing the remaining estimated 700,000 slaves, who would owe no compensation to their former owners. The decree was known as the Lei Áurea (Golden Law), and it simply stated the following: "From this date, slavery is declared abolished in Brazil. All dispositions to the contrary are revoked."

To defend her controversial decision, Princess Isabel was quoted as saying, in Roderick Barman's book, *Princess Isabel of Brazil: Gender and Power in the Nineteenth Century*.

"How did the abolitionist viewpoint gain ground so quickly in me? The concept, already innate within me, was intrinsically humanitarian, moral, generous, great, and supported by the Church. Slavery was essentially an imposition. The owners had profited too long from this imposition. What if they had paid wages from the start? It is true that if they had, they would have had resources they could have disposed of, and thus done some would not have collapsed so helplessly. However, the evil was done, and it could not help but be eradicated."

Despite having passed such an important law, Isabel would do little else as regent before her father returned. Pedro II's return was avidly celebrated by the people of Brazil. However, many historians believe he was so openly supported at this time because he was clearly going to be Brazil's final emperor. Brazil's monarchy had been losing power for decades, and Princess Isabel, the heir to the throne, had not been raised and prepared to be the next ruler.

Brazil's growing contempt for the empire, along with Isabel's inexperience, gender, and her controversial marriage to a Frenchman, would all lead to the empire's downfall. Isabel's husband, Gaston, Count of Eu, recounted this in a letter he wrote to his father after the return of Pedro II in 1888:

"The avidity and the enthusiasm of the public for the Emperor have been very great, more even more marked, it appears to me, than on previous arrivals. But it is a totally personal homage; because, as I think I have already written, the republican creed has made since his departure last year enormous advances that impress everybody; and, notwithstanding the economic prosperity during the present year, never, for the past 40 years, has the situation of the Brazilian monarchy appeared more shaky than today."

The Collapse of the Brazilian Monarchy

Brazil's second emperor would be its last. Since Pedro II had known a revolution was coming for years, he did not try and stop the military coup in 1889.

Today, Brazil is considered to be a struggling country, despite its industrialization and the fact it was once a powerhouse country. Most historians consider Brazil's fall in reputation to be a result of this military coup.

Despite never wanting the job, Pedro II helped rapidly develop Brazil. During his reign, the population more than tripled; there was an estimated fourteen million people in Brazil at the end of the 19th century. Part of this was a result of his pro-immigration policies.

The economy and establishment of infrastructures followed a similar pattern, with exports and profits growing more than ten times during his reign. Railroads were built throughout his empire, connecting more than eight thousand kilometers of the massive country that had once been considered uninhabitable.

But however successful Pedro II may have been in his reign, the population of Brazil was still frustrated with the royal family. When the military staged a coup, Pedro II, who was too old, ill, and loyal to Brazil to battle his own people, allowed the military to take over without a fight.

The revolutionary group that led the coup was made up of rich Brazilian farm owners, the military, and the church. This movement was also supported by Brazil's growing middle class, who were mostly living in the cities. The frustration with the royal family grew hand in hand with the coffee industry in Brazil, as many believed the imperial system was outdated and that a government with a capitalist system would better suit Brazil's political climate at the time.

Many viewed Pedro II as simply a figurehead since the Brazilian elites held all the power and had been the real players who helped develop Brazil. Pedro II is even quoted as saying, "Let the country govern itself as it thinks best and consider right whoever may be right." Perhaps this was because he never truly wanted to be the ruler. Regardless, when the bloodless military coup occurred on November 15th, 1889, Pedro II and his family went into exile in

Europe, a move that Pedro II welcomed with open arms.

Although Pedro II did not believe the military regime would be in the best interest of Brazil, especially when examples of similar failures had happened all over South America, he allowed the transition to take place without objection. Despite the emperor's successes, many historians believe Pedro II's passivity allowed the revolutionary movement to take place. His trust in Brazil's military and local governments, which he essentially groomed to take over, also led to Brazil's downfall.

Regardless, the late 1880s were revolutionary for Brazil, with 1888 marking the abolition of slavery, an institution that had been closely tied with the nation's economy, society, and beliefs, and 1889 bringing the end of the monarchy. For better or for worse, the 1890s and onward would mark the emergence of a "new" Brazil.

Chapter 9 – The Formation and Development of the Brazilian Republic in the Late 19th and Early 20th Centuries (1889–1950)

The First President of Brazil

While there had been many supporters of the military coup, one true leader emerged from the movement: Manuel Deodoro da Fonseca. Following in his father's footsteps, Fonseca joined the Brazilian military and earned recognition and a rank for his service in the War of the Triple Alliance. In the next decade, he rose both as a military leader and an administrative leader and would be considered by many (and certainly by himself) to be the second leading military figure of Brazil, only after Duke of Caxias, Luís Alves de Lima e Silva.

After helping to lead the military coup in 1889 and spending some time as the provisional leader of Brazil, Fonseca was officially elected as Brazil's first president in February 1891. That same month, the Constituent Assembly, which had elected him as president, finished writing a new Brazilian constitution, which they had begun immediately writing after the military coup.

Brazil's 1891 Constitution

The new Brazilian Constitution of 1891 was closely modeled after the Constitution of the United States, which was obvious in many aspects. First, the Brazilian Constitution officially declared Brazil as an independent, republican federation, which would be made up of twenty self-governing states. The presidents of the states, who would later become known as governors, would have fixed terms and be elected, as would the state senators and deputies, who would represent their state in federal affairs. The president of Brazil would also have a fixed term of only four years and, unlike US presidents, could not be immediately reelected. All literate men had the right to vote for their executive leaders.

Like the United States, power was separated into three branches: legislative, executive, and judicial. The Brazilian Constitution also separated the church and state, protected more liberties, and abolished the death penalty.

Overall, the Constitution of 1891 did not really work for the Brazilians and would be nowhere near as long-lasting as the US Constitution. The Brazilian Constitution's failure was due to multiple factors, including the states holding too much power and the political leaders not believing or following the constitution. Fonseca is a good example of this. Immediately after the release of the Brazilian Constitution, he attempted to rule by decree rather than get approval from the legislative powers. He leaned toward tyranny, and many viewed his decisions as ineffective.

By the end of Fonseca's first year as president, he was forced to resign, which would just be the beginning of Brazil's political instability following the monarchy's collapse. Fonseca was succeeded by his vice president, Floriano Peixoto, who ruled with similar authoritarian views. During his few years as president, Peixoto's military past would help him suppress many revolutions, which were still prevalent.

Brazil's Civilian Leaders and the Economy

While a military coup had ousted the emperor and transformed Brazil into a republic, the Brazilians did not want the military involved in government. There had been too many examples of military governments failing in neighboring countries, and both of Brazil's first two presidents, Fonseca and Peixoto, brought this fear to life since they ruled authoritatively. The people knew their ruling styles could easily develop into a dictatorship.

Peixoto managed to control the various revolutions calling for a change in government. Some rebels demanded a return to the monarchy, but most simply requested a civilian leader. When the majority of Brazil was finally deemed "peaceful" enough to no longer be run by the military, the latter demand would finally come true. In 1894, Prudente de Morais would not only be Brazil's first civilian leader voted in by direct popular ballot but also the first in the long line of what would become known as "coffee presidents."

Prudente de Morais was born in São Paulo and grew up alongside the coffee industry, which developed in the state. Before becoming president, he proved his administrative skills and popularity by serving as governor of São Paulo.

Prudente de Morais and the next string of debatably forgettable "coffee presidents" managed to maintain peace in Brazil. However, their main focus was Brazil's coffee industry. While Brazil's economy would be successful in the next decades, with some diversification in the sugar, cotton, tobacco, cocoa, and rubber industries, the presidents mainly focused on coffee and did little to advance Brazil politically.

Brazil's Immigration Pre-World War I

One aspect of Brazil's culture that cannot be ignored from the late 19th and early 20th centuries was immigration. In the decade after the creation of the Republic of Brazil, the nation let in more than three times as many immigrants as before. There would be a massive boom of Italian immigrants. Brazil has the most people of Italian heritage outside of Italy, as it is home to more than thirty million Italian Brazilians.

Immigrants arrived in Brazil from all over the world, but they mainly came from Europe and settled in states with growing economies. From the 1880s to the 1910s, São Paulo experienced massive population growth. Another example of this is in the Amazon River Basin, specifically the city of Manaus, which became the center of Brazil's rubber industry. The previously isolated city of Manaus suddenly got electricity, transit, and incredible buildings.

This effect was even more apparent in the capital city of Rio de Janeiro, which, under the leadership of Mayor Francisco Pereira Passos, was demolished and rebuilt into the iconic city known today. Of course, the demolition of Rio, which began with Passos and would continue over the following century in other cities as well, displaced those who had been living there before, specifically impoverished communities.

Brazil's Impoverished Communities and Struggles with Racism

This reconstruction left many Afro-Brazilians forced to move into cortiços, which translates essentially to ghettos. Cortiços were cramped small apartments with poor sanitation that people could rent at low prices.

Although the cortiços were more affordable than other apartments in Brazil, impoverished communities usually struggled to keep up with rent (largely due to pay/opportunity/education inequalities), so behind each of those tightly packed doors was usually more than one family splitting the rent. In the yards, one could see clothes hung up to dry. Education was not really accessible in the early 1900s, especially for those in impoverished communities.

While slavery had been abolished and Brazil had been welcoming immigrants in the decades before World War I, racism was alive in the Republic of Brazil. Unlike in the United States, where the races were segregated and intermarriage was illegal in the 20th century, in Brazil, white people's "defense" from the other races was not avoidance but "whitening." From the start of Brazil's history, miscegenation and Europeanization had been common, which led to the creation of a distinctive "Brazilian" race, and not much had changed centuries later. A passage from the 1911 novel, *A Esfinge* (*The Sphinx*), written by Brazilian author Júlio Afrânio Peixoto, demonstrates this view well:

"The slow fusion of still imperfect mixtures, the repeated cultural selection, the forced discipline of social organization will make this mass into a strong, happy, and healthy population because the dominant traits are good."

When US President Theodore Roosevelt visited Brazil in 1913, he also made note of this "whitening" process:

"In Brazil, the idea looked forward to is the disappearance of the Negro question through the disappearance of the Negro himself, that is, through his gradual absorption into the white race."

This whitening process, of course, affected the African Brazilians and the indigenous Brazilians. With all of the immigration and expansion in the 20th century, the indigenous tribes of Brazil suffered worse than ever before. While the Europeans had been cruel to the original Brazilians since they first arrived, their cruelty by perpetrating the genocide of the indigenous people has only become known recently. Over the course of the 20th century, it is estimated the indigenous population of Brazil dropped by around 80 percent, mostly through wars and disease.

Disease also ran rampant through the cortiços, affecting the impoverished communities, which, according to government officials, were ruining Brazil's reputation abroad. Officials did not seem to particularly care about the Brazilian people who were sick; they were more concerned about how Rio looked to trade partners and immigrants.

If Brazil was going to compete with the powerhouse countries, it had to be respectable and civilized. A mass clean-up of Brazil's cities, specifically Rio de Janeiro, commenced around 1900, which partially included the demolition of houses deemed unsanitary; thus, the impoverished communities living in cortiços were rehomed again. Pools were shut down, and infrastructures were sanitized.

The sanitization was controversial, but dissatisfaction reached an all-time high when smallpox came around. The government planned to force everyone to be vaccinated. In November 1904, there was a massive, violent, destructive uprising called the Revolta da Vacina (the Vaccine Revolt) in Rio de Janeiro, which aimed to defend the liberties of those who did not want to be vaccinated. The vaccination mandate was repealed, but the clean-up of Rio continued at an exponential rate, forcing thousands out of their "unsanitary" homes.

With many people looking for places to live, the quick construction began on Rio de Janeiro's iconic favelas, which is a somewhat offensive term for a working-class area, similar to a slum. The favelas were packed tightly together. They were constructed without government approval or planning and would continue to be built over the course of the 20th century to keep up with the growing population, even after their hygiene and safety became a concern.

An image of favelas.
chensiyuan, CC BY-SA 4.0 <https://creativecommons.org/licenses/by-sa/4.0>, via Wikimedia Commons;
https://commons.wikimedia.org/wiki/File:1_rocinha_favela_closeup.JPG

As demonstrated by the vaccination campaign to fight disease and the necessity of the favelas, Rio de Janeiro's (and Brazil's) rapid modernization proved to be disastrous for the people. To make matters worse, the exponential population growth in Rio caused food shortages, and unemployment was at an all-time high before World War I. Overall, the standard of living in Brazil, for anyone who was not affluent, was unacceptable.

Brazil's Foreign Affairs and Wars in the Early 20th Century

In the early 20th century, Brazil continued to expand, acquiring more land for its growing population. Although the nation gained more territory than France during this time, the strength of its army and allies allowed it to seize land without many consequences. While Brazil's alliance with Britain continued into the 20th century, Brazil's presidents focused more on the relationship with the nearby powerhouse of the United States, explaining why President Theodore Roosevelt paid Brazil a visit during this time.

Although Brazilians were somewhat divided on their beliefs during World War I, it was ultimately their alliances that led them to join the Allies. Overall, Brazil would stay mostly uninvolved in the Great War, although it finally sent a small force to France in 1918, three years after the war had begun. This was partly due to the war's lack of relevance to the Brazilian people and partly because Brazil was dealing with its own internal wars during this time.

The Contestado War

From 1912 to 1916, two-thirds of Brazil's army was involved in the Contestado War, which, as the name indicates, was fought over contested land in southern Brazil around the Argentinian border. The war was so bloody and intense that even women from nearby regions joined the battle. In the end, it was realized that autonomy did not work in rural states where the population was spread out.

The Contestado War went to great lengths in convincing the population that the military was necessary and that a civilian government was not effective. After the war ended, members of the military ended up staying in the region to maintain order. This belief can be demonstrated in a quote from *A Defesa Nacional*, a military magazine: "May the example of army bravery and death in the Contestado serve as a lesson to the timid and indifferent citizens of Brazil."

The military's power was divisive in Brazil; however, many believed only the military could help fix the issues present in the nation. This sentiment was shown in a speech given to law students in 1915. Renowned Brazilian writer Olavo Bilac said, "What is universal military service? It is the complete triumph of democracy; the leveling of social classes; the school of order, discipline, and cohesion; the laboratory of self dignity and patriotism ... The cities are full of unshod vagrants and ragamuffins ... For these dregs of society, the barracks would be a salvation. The barracks are an admirable filter in which men cleanse and purify themselves: they emerge conscientious and dignified Brazilians." Ironically, Bilac never served in the military himself and used to be openly against conscription.

Tenentismo in the 1920s

Nearly every period in Brazil's history can be marked by public dissatisfaction, and the early 20th century was no different. By the 1920s, public frustration with the "coffee presidents," especially amongst the middle working class of Brazil, had reached an all-time high. This sentiment was shared by many of the younger members of the military, who were known as *tenentes* (lieutenants). Starting in 1922, these frustrated junior officers would stage various uprisings and even an attempted coup, with the goal of putting an end to the civilian government that had been dominated by the elite Brazilian coffee plantation owners since the creation of the republic.

The rest of the 1920s were turbulent, with the tenentes' revolutionary movement, known as Tenentismo, gaining traction and getting more and more extreme. By the mid-1920s, Tenentismo had transformed into a nationalistic ideology that called for the replacement of the government by the military. While Tenentismo was a modern ideology that demanded many necessary changes, such as the establishment of minimum wage, fair working conditions and hours, more accessible education, and a modernized economy, it was also somewhat regressive, as it highlighted the need for a centralized, authoritative government. The common belief of the tenentes was that the military's complete authoritative control was necessary to reform Brazil. Once the necessary changes had been made, the nation could return to a constitutional rule.

It must be noted that despite the fact the middle class of Brazil was also frustrated with the government, it was mostly only young, middle-class military officers who supported Tenentismo's extreme ideologies.

Regardless of the coffee presidents' unpopularity, the 1920s would finish with the Great Depression, which tanked coffee prices, ultimately forcing Brazil to revitalize its economy and government. Public frustration would reach new heights in 1930 when the president at the time, Washington Luís, attempted to choose his own successor. It was at this point that all of the frustrated people of Brazil found common ground to unite and revolt.

The losing candidate in the unfair 1930 election, Getúlio Vargas, led a military coup, which made the requests of the Tenentismo movement come to life, turning the military into a political entity and putting Brazil under an authoritative military rule.

Getúlio Vargas

After leading the Brazilian Revolution of 1930, Getúlio Vargas claimed the role of "provisionary president." In other words, he became the dictator of Brazil.

Like the rest of the world at this time, Brazil struggled economically during the early 1930s. With much of the power being taken away from the previously sovereign states, Brazilians were once again frustrated, which was demonstrated by the many violent revolts in which they took part.

To placate the population, Vargas reinstated a Constituent Assembly, which began writing a new constitution, one that would at least pacify the population while he "dealt" with Brazil's issues and remained in power. The constitution was finished in 1934, and one of its important highlights included taking power away from the states and giving it to the central government; in other words, the power would be given to Vargas himself. Other notable changes in the new constitution included giving everyone in Brazil over eighteen the right to vote (including all sexes and races) and nationalized industries, such as mining and newspapers, with the hope of boosting Brazil's economy since it had been entirely dependent on coffee. The Constituent Assembly also voted Vargas as president of Brazil.

Brazil's Estado Nôvo

The 1934 Constitution ensured that, once again, the president would be limited to a four-year term. Of course, with Brazil's dissatisfaction with the current military government, Vargas knew he would not be voted in again. Thus, in 1937, a year before his term was meant to end, Vargas amended the constitution to stay in power, making him the dictator of Brazil once again. Not only was the right to vote taken from the public, but so were many other basic liberties, which Vargas explained away by claiming Brazil was in a state of emergency.

During this period (between 1937 and 1945), Vargas proclaimed Brazil as Estado Nôvo ("new state"). Although Brazilians were known to be against authoritative governments and feared a dictatorship, Brazil was in a crisis, and Vargas promised to reform the nation. Civilians were less scared of Vargas than what would happen if his administration disappeared, especially with the rise of communism in Brazil. Many state governments reluctantly gave up their powers to Vargas to avoid a bloody civil war. Vargas ultimately had more power than Brazil's emperors ever had.

During the Estado Nôvo period, Brazil experienced a strange movement of growth and regression. The economy grew and diversified, minimum wages were established, and working conditions were improved. However, journalists were censored, all political parties were dissolved, and education was segregated.

World War II

Tenentismo had created a deep divide in the Brazilian military, as many young officers stopped respecting older, higher-ranking officers who were not as supportive of the military government. Regardless of the breaks within the military, the 1930s marked a period of support for the military, as recruitment reached an all-time high, especially toward the end of the decade with the start of World War II.

Despite the poor public opinion of Vargas, the dictator had kept good relations with Brazil's allies, specifically the United States. In 1936, US President Franklin Delano Roosevelt visited Brazil. After his visit, he said, "It has been a great privilege for me to make the acquaintance of your President. I have had the privilege of knowing some of his family before today and I hope that in the not too distant future we shall be able to welcome President Vargas at Washington as a visitor in the United States."

Many believe the US president's visit to Brazil was mostly about strengthening the two nations' relationship in preparation for World War II. Although it would take until 1942, Brazil finally joined the Allies, declaring war against Nazi Germany. In 1944, Brazil actually sent a force to Italy, and the strength of the Brazilian military gained global attention.

During the early 1940s, Brazil's previously fractured military healed its wounds by fighting together in World War II. They also hated President Vargas, whose absolute dictatorship had gone too far. Two months after the end of World War II, after the military had returned home and had time to discuss things, Brazil's military staged a coup. Vargas relinquished the "presidency" on October

29th, 1945, and two months later, Brazil held elections to reinstate its first president since the beginning of the Vargas era.

General Eurico Gaspar Dutra's Presidency

In December 1945, with the support of Vargas, General Eurico Gaspar Dutra of the Social Democratic Party of Brazil was elected president. The following year, a new constitution was promulgated, which renamed the Republic of Brazil to the United States of Brazil (Estados Unidos do Brazil). The highlights of this new constitution included restoring the liberties Brazilians enjoyed before Vargas's military dictatorship, reducing the president's power and term, returning power to the states, allowing all political beliefs and parties to be legal, and opposing censorship of any kind.

Since Dutra previously served as Brazil's minister of war, his presidency was supported by and focused on the military. Although Dutra would help to restore democracy in Brazil, he was not able to make as many positive changes as his successor, which was especially obvious in the economy, which did not profit from the war as much as other nations.

Although Dutra was unpopular, he managed to improve Brazil in less noticeable ways, such as expanding the railroads and electricity and constructing thousands of new schools throughout Brazil. That being said, in 1950, with Brazilians once again frustrated, Dutra's five-year term came to an end, and a new public election was held in which Vargas was reelected (this time by the people) as Brazil's president.

Chapter 10 – Brazil in the Second Half of the 20th Century (1950–2000)

Vargas's Return to Leadership

Vargas was officially reinstated as Brazil's president on January 31st, 1951, this time by popular vote. Despite the fact the people had chosen to elect Vargas, there was still a good portion of the population, specifically those in the military, who were fearful that Vargas's presidency would once again become a dictatorship.

Though Dutra is considered not to have accomplished much during his time as president, the constitution written during his presidency is what kept Vargas in his place during his second term. Ironically, many Brazilians considered the constitution to be too strict and even went as far as to say it weakened Vargas's potential to make real necessary changes as president.

Regardless, Brazil was once again divided. Vargas was almost equally loved and hated, and similarly, Congress was split, making it difficult for Vargas to pass many laws. Vargas struggled to improve Brazil's economy, and unemployment, inflation, and debt continued to rise. Brazil was split on how to fix the economy. Many believed the government should get more involved, while others believed Brazil should lean toward capitalism and depend on private companies to help the economy.

In the early 1950s, Vargas took many measures to try and solve the economic issues, including establishing a national petroleum company, Petrobras, and raising the minimum wage. Unfortunately, the minimum wage was raised too quickly, which led to greater inflation and many uprisings around Brazil.

By August 1954, Vargas's term came to a disastrous end when it was discovered his government had hired assassins to kill high-ranking officers and a newspaper editor. Further investigations uncovered rampant corruption in Vargas's government. Both the public and the military demanded that Vargas resign, but the turmoil culminated when Brazil's president ended his own life at the end of August.

President Kubitschek (Brazil Post-Vargas)

Vargas's vice president finished out his predecessor's term until a new election could be held in October 1955. Juscelino Kubitschek would just barely win the vote, despite being considered by many to be a more radical heir to Vargas. President Kubitschek aligned with the Brazilian people's nationalistic views and believed, much like the early leaders of Brazil, that the nation could and should become a powerhouse.

Kubitschek focused much of his energy on reconstructing Brazil. During his five years in office, he oversaw the construction of highways, hydroelectric power plants, and an entirely new capital city, Brasília. The construction of Brasília finished in 1960, and it was nearly one thousand kilometers away from the nation's previous capital, Rio de Janeiro. While some saw the project to be a waste of time, the majority of Brazilians supported it, believing it could help Brazil gain positive attention and become somewhat of a symbol of Brazil's bright future. Kubitschek also helped fund and strengthen the military and the automotive industry.

Although Kubitschek's motto, "Fifty Years' Progress in Five," was an exaggeration, he helped Brazil make great leaps forward in its reputation abroad. That being said, life for the inhabitants of Brazil did not improve much, as debt increased in the 1950s, and the living conditions remained mostly the same. Within thirty years, Brazil's population more than doubled, and by 1960, it had a population of seventy million people. The nation was growing at exponential rates. Brazil diversified its economy, yet debt and inflation kept real change from occurring.

Presidents Quadros and Goulart

Following the end of Kubitschek's presidency, there was little stability in office, as Kubitschek's successor, Jânio Quadros, resigned after around seven months. In September 1961, Quadros was replaced by his vice president, João Goulart, who was a political confidant of Vargas. Goulart's relationship with Vargas led to almost everyone not trusting him, as is demonstrated in a telegram sent by the ambassador of Brazil in 1964:

"My considered conclusion is that Goulart is now definitely engaged on campaign to seize dictatorial power, accepting the active collaboration of the Brazilian Communist Party, and of other radical left revolutionaries to this end."

This fear expressed by the ambassador was shared by the general public. So, once again, Brazil experienced a period of incessant uprisings. Despite making some positive changes in Brazil, the turmoil culminated in 1964 when Goulart's supporters tried to defend the president by striking and mutinying. Despite breaking contracts and laws, they were not punished, which led to chaos. Goulart eventually fled to Uruguay, and the military stepped in to take control of Brazil.

Return to Brazil's Military Government (1964-1985)

After the collapse of the empire, Brazilians had high hopes the nation would be able to achieve a modern, civilized democracy. However, Brazil's 20th century was defined by constant political instability. After flip-flopping between authoritative military rulers and democratic presidents, the nation returned to a military dictatorship in 1964. This time, it would be for twenty-one years.

After President Goulart's downfall, the population wanted a democratically elected civilian president. However, the nation was greatly divided, and any elected candidate would have likely suffered a revolution. Thus, Humberto de Alencar Castelo Branco, Brazil's chief of staff, became a dictator. Like Vargas, he promised to reinstate democracy once Brazil was reformed and at peace.

Despite the fact most of Brazil hated Goulart, they were greatly dissatisfied with the new military system. Since the beginning of the empire, it seems Brazilians were constantly disappointed with their leadership, perhaps because the nation is so large, populated, and spread out, making it divided. It seemed for the past century that Brazil would stage revolutions, a revolutionary group would oust the leader and replace them, and the pattern would restart. No matter who was in charge or what system was in place, Brazilians seemed to be dissatisfied, perhaps because the nation was ideologically advanced but behind most "civilized" nations that had better living conditions and more stable governments. Brazilian liberties were constantly changing, and during the military dictatorship, two more constitutions would be promulgated.

While the five Brazilian dictators who were in power during the twenty-one-year military period kept promising Brazil would return to a democratic system once peace was achieved, they struggled to suppress the endless rebellions.

Once again, Brazil was in a period of advancements and regressions. The military dictators built factories, highways, and schools, but without the internal funding to do so, the nation went into debt, borrowing money from its allies, specifically the United States. In the 1970s, Brazil was struggling. However, its economic issues were hidden from the world so Brazil could look like a powerhouse nation on the world stage. While Brazil's economy grew during the military dictatorship, the majority of the population was not seeing any effects of this growth. Rural regions barely developed, and a majority of the population was impoverished, illiterate, and living unhygienically. This period in the 1970s was ironically dubbed the "Economic Miracle."

Public Frustration and an Attempted Return to Democracy

By the end of the 1970s, other nations had realized Brazil's true position. They were able to see past the image Brazil had been putting out internationally. After receiving worldwide criticism, Brazil even renounced its longtime military relationship with the United States. Brazilian leaders realized something had to change, and the dictators gradually allowed for more democracy and liberties.

When the final military dictator, João Figueiredo, took control in 1979, he resolved to return Brazil to a democratic nation. Figueiredo tried to focus on undoing some of his predecessors' negative actions; for example, he returned liberties that had been taken away from the Brazilian people and reestablished relations with foreign nations, which would be necessary to help improve Brazil's economy. To combat the record debt the military dictatorship had accumulated, Figueiredo invested in nearly every industry, from petroleum and electricity to arms and automobiles. While Brazil's economy slightly improved during the early 1980s, inflation ensured no Brazilians felt the positive effects. The nation remained in an economic crisis.

In 1983, Figueiredo fell sick. For the following year, the nation would not have any real political leadership. The Brazilians were tired of military rule, and they used Figueiredo's absence as an opportunity to demand change. Revolutions broke out all over the nation, many of which were led by Brazil's college students, a section of society that had been politically active since the 1960s.

Although Brazilians demanded the next leader be elected by the people, Congress did not grant their wish. However, it did allow an electoral college to vote in the population's favorite contender, Tancredo Neves, for the presidency. Despite not being able to vote, the population was ecstatic to finally have a fair, democratic president again.

However, if the past century was any indication of Brazil's luck, things would not go as planned. Neves, who had been sick, suddenly died the same month he was officially elected. Instead, his vice president, José Sarney, a renowned supporter of the military regime, took the vacant position, stealing Brazil's chance for democracy. Although a new election should have been called after Neves's death, Sarney took control and remained in power for the following five years.

Brazil's Politics in the New Republic (1985-1990)

Sarney and the subsequent leaders would struggle to satisfy the Brazilians' requests and needs. Changes were unstable, and reforms rarely lasted. While Sarney managed to solve the nation's inflation rate, by the end of the 1980s, inflation would be back at an all-time high. A new constitution in 1988 took more power away from the president. Laws had to be passed through not only the executive branch but also the legislative and sometimes judicial branches. While the 1988 Constitution would be amended many times after, it is the constitution Brazil still uses today.

Although Sarney was not technically voted in by the people, his rule ended Brazil's military rule and launched Brazil into its modern age, also known as the Sixth Brazilian Republic or New Republic. Sarney was popular at first, but by the end of his term, the people were dissatisfied. By 1990, inflation was once again at a record high, violent uprisings were occurring all over the nation, and new government corruption scandals were being revealed monthly.

After the 1988 Constitution launched Brazil into its renewed democratic era, the nation prepared to oust Sarney. This time, a coup would not be necessary since popular elections were being held the following year.

Brazil in the 1990s

Brazil would still be politically unstable in the following decade. Although the constitution remained intact, there would be no elected president for a time. Government corruption almost impeached the first president voted in after Sarney. After his resignation, the vice president temporarily acted as leader until the next election.

In 1994, Fernando Henrique Cardoso was elected president. He made great strides in addressing Brazil's inequality and economic issues. His constitutionally-allowed term ended on an overall positive note in 2002, and the nation voted for its next leader. This would be the first time Brazil had been able to elect two leaders in a row in nearly half a decade.

Overall, the final decade of the 20th century would be a transitionary period for Brazil. So many reforms occurred that an entire book could be written about just one state or city during the 1990s. The nation spent the decade trying to reach some semblance of equality and freedom and overcome its economic crisis and crippling class gaps.

So far, the 21st century has been spent in a similar manner. Though Brazil has made extreme progress in the past quarter-century, it never quite reached the powerhouse status Brazilians believed it could. With less dramatic but still relevant political instability, further financial crises, and a good portion of the population living under the poverty line, Brazil is still trying to overcome the turbulence of its 20th century.

Conclusion

Despite many improvements being made to Brazil in recent history, the nation and its people still suffer from many of the issues that have plagued it since its independence from Portugal. The educational system is not up to par with other nations around the world, corruption still runs rampant within the government, and the divide between the economic classes is massive. Today, Brazil is the world's leading coffee, soybean, beef, and tobacco exporters and one of the top exporters of sugar and iron. Yet, similar to the early days of Brazil when sugar plantation owners and coffee farmers ruled the land, the profits of these industries are almost entirely directed to the already-rich Brazilian elites.

Brazil is the fifth-most inhabited country in the world. It is in the top ten global GDPs and is extremely vast and resource-rich. Yet, it never reached its superpower nation status. While some political scientists believe the nation could eventually transition into a superpower, it would have to overcome fundamental political, economic, and social issues that have been ingrained into Brazilian culture since its discovery.

Inequality and racism are still extremely prevalent in the nation, even after decades of reforms. While the indigenous population of Brazil finally began to rise in numbers by the end of the 20th century, the several hundred tribes that live within the nation are still struggling to keep their land because of Brazil's economic development and resource hunting.

It must be noted that despite all of the aspects of Brazil's history that can be viewed as negative, the people of Brazil managed to survive the turbulence and develop an extremely rich, creative, and distinctive culture. While intermarriage and immigration created a unique Brazilian ethnicity that is different from any other nation, Brazil is a massive territory, and each region has its own ethnic breakdown, culture, and customs.

While much of Brazilian culture is inherited from its Portuguese roots, most obviously its religion, language, and some traditions, indigenous and African influences completely altered the culture. Brazil's culture is almost incomparable to that of Portugal. This distinction from Portugal is obvious in its most iconic artists, who write, illustrate, and perform art with themes that could only have been written by Brazilians. An example of a custom unique to Brazil is Carnival, a four-day holiday that combines art, dancing, magnificent costumes, and customs from its African population with a Roman Catholic festival from its Portuguese heritage.

The early emergence of economic disparity resulted in mass poverty that went largely unchecked. Impoverished communities were forced to fend for themselves with little government help until the 21st century, explaining why the nation is still known for crime and danger today. However, overall, Brazil is a vibrant nation with a rich culture that is still trying to overcome its turbulent political and economic past.

Here's another book by Captivating History that you might like

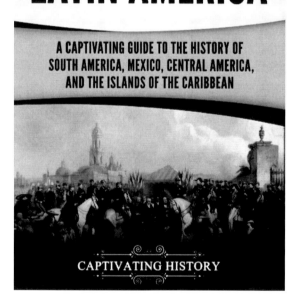

Free Bonus from Captivating History (Available for a Limited time)

Hi History Lovers!

Now you have a chance to join our exclusive history list so you can get your first history ebook for free as well as discounts and a potential to get more history books for free! Simply visit the link below to join.

Captivatinghistory.com/ebook

Also, make sure to follow us on Facebook, Twitter and Youtube by searching for Captivating History.

Bibliography

Academic Dictionaries and Encyclopedias. (2022). Iberian Union. Retrieved August 2022, from https://en-academic.com/dic.nsf/enwiki/800026

Academic Dictionaries and Encyclopedias. (2022). Treaty of the Hague (1661). Retrieved August 2022, from https://en-academic.com/dic.nsf/enwiki/4169146

Alden, D. (1963). The Population of Brazil in the Late Eighteenth Century: A Preliminary Study. *Hispanic American Historical Review, 43* (2): 173-205. doi:10.1215/00182168-43.2.173

Barman, R. J. (2002). *Princess Isabel of Brazil Gender and Power in the Nineteenth Century.* Wilmington, Del: SR Books.

Bartos, N. (2017, August 15). Circles of mystery: Strange ancient earthworks in Brazil's Amazonian Rainforest. Retrieved August 2022, from https://www.world-archaeology.com/issues/circles-of-mystery-strange-ancient-earthworks-in-brazils-amazonian-rainforest/

Biello, D. (2008, August 28). Ancient amazon actually highly urbanized. Retrieved August 2022, from https://www.scientificamerican.com/article/lost-amazon-cities/

Blakemore, E. (2021, May 03). New discovery shows Amazon jungle once home to many millions. Retrieved August 2022, from https://www.nationalgeographic.com/history/article/amazon-jungle-ancient-population-satellite-computer-model

Boxer, C. R. (1969). Brazilian Gold and British Traders in the First Half of the Eighteenth Century. *Hispanic American Historical Review, 49* (3): 454-472. doi:10.1215/00182168-49.3.454

Brazil Chamber of Deputies - National Congress Palace. (2022). Pedro de Araújo Lima. Retrieved August 2022, from https://www2.camara.leg.br/a-camara/conheca/presidentes/pedro_lima2.html

The Brazilian Report. (2020, May 13). Slavery in Brazil. Retrieved August 2022, from https://www.wilsoncenter.org/blog-post/slavery-brazil

Britannica, The Editors of Encyclopedia. (1998, July 20). Acto Adicional of 1834. Retrieved August 2022, from https://www.britannica.com/topic/Acto-Adicional-of-1834

Britannica, The Editors of Encyclopedia. (1998, July 20). Strangford Treaty. Retrieved August 2022, from https://www.britannica.com/event/Strangford-Treaty

Britannica, The Editors of Encyclopedia. (2007, March 9). Tenentismo. Retrieved August 2022, from https://www.britannica.com/event/Tenentismo

Britannica, The Editors of Encyclopedia. (2014, June 6). War of the triple alliance. Retrieved August 2022, from https://www.britannica.com/event/War-of-the-Triple-Alliance

Britannica, The Editors of Encyclopedia. (2016, July 25). List of Spanish monarchs. Retrieved August 2022, from https://www.britannica.com/topic/list-of-Spanish-monarchs-2070695

Britannica, The Editors of Encyclopedia. (2016, June 16). Pernambuco. Retrieved August 2022, from https://www.britannica.com/place/Pernambuco

Britannica, The Editors of Encyclopedia. (2020, January 18). Maria II. Retrieved August 2022, from https://www.britannica.com/biography/Maria-II

Britannica, The Editors of Encyclopedia. (2021, January 1). Napoleonic wars. Retrieved August 2022, from https://www.britannica.com/event/Napoleonic-Wars

Britannica, The Editors of Encyclopedia. (2021, May 5). Pedro I. Retrieved August 2022, from https://www.britannica.com/biography/Pedro-I

Britannica, The Editors of Encyclopedia. (2022). Colonization of the Americas. Retrieved August 2022, from https://kids.britannica.com/students/article/colonization-of-the-Americas/272832

Britannica, The Editors of Encyclopedia. (2022, April 10). Philip IV. Retrieved August 2022, from https://www.britannica.com/biography/Philip-IV-king-of-Spain-and-Portugal

Britannica, The Editors of Encyclopedia. (2022, April 2). José Bonifácio de Andrada e Silva. Retrieved August 2022, from https://www.britannica.com/biography/Jose-Bonifacio-de-Andrada-e-Silva

Britannica, The Editors of Encyclopedia. (2022, August 19). Manuel Deodoro da Fonseca. Retrieved August 2022, from https://www.britannica.com/biography/Manuel-Deodoro-da-Fonseca

Britannica, The Editors of Encyclopedia. (2022, January 1). Martín Alonso Pinzón and Vicente Yáñez Pinzón. Retrieved August 2022, from https://www.britannica.com/biography/Martin-Alonso-Pinzon

Britannica, The Editors of Encyclopedia. (2022, January 1). Tomé de Sousa. Retrieved August 2022, from https://www.britannica.com/biography/Tome-de-Sousa

Britannica, The Editors of Encyclopedia. (2022, January 14). Slash-and-burn agriculture. Retrieved August 2022, from https://www.britannica.com/topic/slash-and-burn-agriculture

Britannica, The Editors of Encyclopedia. (2022, July 17). Martim Afonso de Sousa. Retrieved August 2022, from https://www.britannica.com/biography/Martim-Afonso-de-Sousa

Britannica, The Editors of Encyclopedia. (2022, July 20). Francisco solano lópez. Retrieved August 2022, from https://www.britannica.com/biography/Francisco-Solano-Lopez

Britannica, The Editors of Encyclopedia. (2022, July 3). Peninsular War. Retrieved August 2022, from https://www.britannica.com/event/Peninsular-War

Britannica, The Editors of Encyclopedia. (2022, June 13). John Maurice of Nassau. Retrieved August 2022, from https://www.britannica.com/biography/John-Maurice-of-Nassau

Britannica, The Editors of Encyclopedia. (2022, June 7). Eurico Gaspar Dutra. Retrieved August 2022, from https://www.britannica.com/biography/Eurico-Gaspar-Dutra

Britannica, The Editors of Encyclopedia. (2022, June 7). John III. Retrieved August 2022, from https://www.britannica.com/biography/John-III-king-of-Portugal

British American Tobacco Brasil. (2022). Souza Cruz - History of Tobacco. Retrieved August 2022, from https://www.batbrasil.com/group/sites/SOU_ASNGAC.nsf/vwPagesWebLive/DO9YDBCK

Brown University. (2022). Abolition. Retrieved August 2022, from https://library.brown.edu/create/fivecenturiesofchange/chapters/chapter-4/abolition/

Brown University. (2022). Bandeirantes, Natives, and Indigenous Slavery. Retrieved August 2022, from
https://library.brown.edu/create/fivecenturiesofchange/

Brown University. (2022). Conflicts with Neighbors to the South. Retrieved August 2022, from
https://library.brown.edu/create/fivecenturiesofchange/chapters/chapter-3/political-instability-in-nineteenth-century-brazil/

Brown University. (2022). Conflicts with Neighbors to the South. Retrieved August 2022, from
https://library.brown.edu/create/fivecenturiesofchange/chapters/chapter-3/political-instability-in-nineteenth-century-brazil/

Brown University. (2022). Cultural Exchange in the Forging of Brazil's Special Relationship with the U.S. Retrieved August 2022, from
https://library.brown.edu/create/fivecenturiesofchange/chapters/chapter-5/media-representations-in-us/

Brown University. (2022). Feitorias and Engenhos: The Changing Economy of Colonial Brazil. Retrieved August 2022, from
https://library.brown.edu/create/fivecenturiesofchange/chapters/chapter-1/feitorias-and-engenhos/

Brown University. (2022). Jânio Quadros. Retrieved August 2022, from
https://library.brown.edu/create/fivecenturiesofchange/chapters/chapter-6/presidents/janio-quadros/

Brown University. (2022). Lead up to the Coup. Retrieved August 2022, from https://library.brown.edu/create/fivecenturiesofchange/lead-up-to-the-coup/

Brown University. (2022). Pedro I and Pedro II. Retrieved August 2022, from
https://library.brown.edu/create/fivecenturiesofchange/chapters/chapter-3/pedro-i-and-pedro-ii/

Brown University. (2022). Return of Vargas. Retrieved August 2022, from
https://library.brown.edu/create/fivecenturiesofchange/chapters/chapter-6/return-of-vargus/

Brown University. (2022). Slavery and Abolition in the 19th Century. Retrieved August 2022, from
https://library.brown.edu/create/fivecenturiesofchange/chapters/chapter-3/slavery-and-aboliton/

Brown University. (2022). The African Slave Trade and Slave Life. Retrieved August 2022, from
https://library.brown.edu/create/fivecenturiesofchange/chapters/chapter-2/african-slavery/

Brown University. (2022). The Jesuit Order in Colonial Brazil. Retrieved August 2022, from https://library.brown.edu/create/fivecenturiesofchange/chapters/chapter-2/the-jesuits/

Brown University. (2022). The Rise of the Military in Politics: From the Old Republic to Estado Novo. Retrieved August 2022, from https://library.brown.edu/create/fivecenturiesofchange/chapters/chapter-5/military-in-politics/

Brown University. (2022). The Vaccine Riots and the Difficulty of Modernization in Rio de Janeiro. Retrieved August 2022, from https://library.brown.edu/create/fivecenturiesofchange/chapters/chapter-5/modernization-in-rio/

Burns, B. E. (1966). *A documentary history of Brazil*. New York: Knopf.

Carrara, A. (2015, January 09). The population of Brazil, 1570-1700: A historiographical review. Retrieved August 2022, from https://www.scielo.br/j/tem/a/ffLjkWqpG7Dz6QQpzrpwvmz/

Conrad, R. (1969). The Contraband Slave Trade to Brazil, 1831-1845. *Hispanic American Historical Review,* 49 (4): 617-638. doi:10.1215/00182168-49.4.617

Davenport, J. (2012, October 12). The Brazilian Gold Rush. Retrieved August 2022, from https://www.miningweekly.com/article/the-brazilian-gold-rush-2012-10-12

DBpedia. (2022). War of Independence of Brazil. Retrieved August 2022, from https://dbpedia.org/page/War_of_Independence_of_Brazil

De Castro, M. F., & Mezzaroba, O. (2018). History of Brazilian Constitutional Law: 1824's Constitution of the Empire of Brasil and the Private Slavery System. *Seqüência: Estudos Jurídicos E Políticos, 39*(78), 11-36. doi:10.5007/2177-7055.2018v39n78p11

Delson, R. (1984). Perspectives on Landscape Change in Brazil. *Journal of Latin American Studies,* 16(01):101 - 125. doi:10.1017/S0022216X00004053

Diamond Museum Amsterdam. (2022). Amsterdam City of Diamonds. Retrieved August 2022, from https://www.diamondmuseum.com/exhibits-themes/city-of-diamonds/city-of-diamonds/

Dockstader, Frederick J. (2021, January 14). Native American art. Retrieved August 2022, from https://www.britannica.com/art/Native-American-art

Driven Coffee Roasters. (2022, May 12). Brazilian coffee: Get to know your coffee origins. Retrieved August 2022, from https://www.drivencoffee.com/blog/brazilian-coffee-origins/

Ducksters. (2022). Brazil History and Timeline Overview. Retrieved August 2022, from https://www.ducksters.com/geography/country/brazil_history_timeline.php

Encyclopedia.com. (2018, May 23). Pedro Álvares Cabral. Retrieved August 2022, from https://www.encyclopedia.com/people/history/explorers-travelers-and-conquerors-biographies/pedro-alvares-cabral

Encyclopedia.com. (2019). Brazil, Constitutions. Retrieved August 2022, from https://www.encyclopedia.com/humanities/encyclopedias-almanacs-transcripts-and-maps/brazil-constitutions

Encyclopedia.com. (2019). Brazil, the Regency. Retrieved August 2022, from https://www.encyclopedia.com/humanities/encyclopedias-almanacs-transcripts-and-maps/brazil-regency

Encyclopedia.com. (2019). Cisplatine Province. Retrieved August 2022, from https://www.encyclopedia.com/humanities/encyclopedias-almanacs-transcripts-and-maps/cisplatine-province

Encyclopedia.com. (2019). Coelho Pereira, Duarte (Late Fifteenth Century–1553 or 1554). Retrieved August 2022, from https://www.encyclopedia.com/humanities/encyclopedias-almanacs-transcripts-and-maps/coelho-pereira-duarte-late-fifteenth-century-1553-or-1554

Encyclopedia.com. (2019). Confederation of the Equator. Retrieved August 2022, from https://www.encyclopedia.com/humanities/encyclopedias-almanacs-transcripts-and-maps/confederation-equator

Encyclopedia.com. (2019). Gold Rushes, Brazil. Retrieved August 2022, from https://www.encyclopedia.com/humanities/encyclopedias-almanacs-transcripts-and-maps/gold-rushes-brazil

Encyclopedia.com. (2019). Marajoara. Retrieved August 2022, from https://www.encyclopedia.com/humanities/encyclopedias-almanacs-transcripts-and-maps/marajoara

Encyclopedia.com. (2019). São Vicente. Retrieved August 2022, from https://www.encyclopedia.com/humanities/encyclopedias-almanacs-transcripts-and-maps/sao-vicente

Geographia. (2006). Brazil - History. Retrieved August 2022, from http://www.geographia.com/brazil/brazihistory.htm

Google Arts & Culture. (2022). Coronation Ceremony of D. Pedro I, Emperor of Brazil. Retrieved August 2022, from https://artsandculture.google.com/asset/coronation-ceremony-of-d-pedro-i-emperor-of-brazil/uQE8ReBA7i1ALA?hl=en

Google Arts and Culture. (2022). Pedro II of Brazil - Google Arts & Culture. Retrieved August 2022, from https://artsandculture.google.com/entity/pedro-ii-of-brazil/m0k_69?hl=en

Government of Brazil. (2021, November 24). Pedro de Araújo Lima. Retrieved August 2022, from https://www.gov.br/funag/pt-br/chdd/historia-diplomatica/ministros-de-estado-das-relacoes-exteriores/pedro-de-araujo-lima

Handbook of Gold Exploration and Evaluation. (2007). Alluvial deposit. Retrieved August 2022, from https://www.sciencedirect.com/topics/engineering/alluvial-deposit

Hirji, Z. (2010, September 09). Nature's cover-up: An ancient Amazonian civilization. Retrieved August 2022, from https://www.nbcnews.com/id/wbna39079905

Huarte, E. Zudaire. (2022, July 18). Gaspar de Guzmán y Pimental, count-duke de olivares. Retrieved August 2022, from https://www.britannica.com/biography/Gaspar-de-Guzman-y-Pimental-conde-duque-de-Olivares

Jamasmie, C. (2015, October 15). Illegal Diamond Mining threatens Brazil's indigenous communities. Retrieved August 2022, from https://www.mining.com/illegal-diamond-mining-threatens-brazils-indigenous-communities/

Kaplan, Marion, Livermore, Harold V., Shercliff, Jose, Smith, Catherine Delano, Amaral, Ilídio Melo Peres do, Opello, Walter C. and Wheeler, Douglas Lanphier. (2022, January 1). Portugal. Retrieved August 2022, from https://www.britannica.com/place/Portugal

Marshall, A. (2022, August 18). What was the Ragamuffin War (1835-1845). Retrieved August 2022, from https://bootcampmilitaryfitnessinstitute.com/2022/08/18/what-was-the-ragamuffin-war-1835-1845/

Moraes, R. B. (1983). Pg 239-240. In *Rubens Borba de Moraes: Anotações de Um Bibliófilo*. Colibris Editora.

Mylan, M. (2006, January 24). Indians of the Amazon Trade and Treasure. Retrieved August 2022, from https://www.pbs.org/frontlineworld/stories/brazil501/indians_trade.html

National Geographic Society. (2022). Jun 7, 1494 CE: Treaty of Tordesillas. Retrieved August 2022, from https://www.nationalgeographic.org/thisday/jun7/treaty-tordesillas/

National Landmark. (2019, January 15). Historic Center of the Town of Olinda, World Heritage Site (Brazil). Retrieved August 2022, from https://lacgeo.com/historic-center-town-olinda-brazil

Pappas, D. (2009, May). The Napoleonic Wars and Brazilian Independence. Retrieved August 2022, from https://www.napoleon-series.org/research/government/Brazil/c_Independence.html

PBS. (2022). The Peninsular War, 1808-1813. Retrieved August 2022, from https://www.pbs.org/empires/napoleon/n_war/campaign/page_9.html

Quinn, M. (2022). Dom Pedro II's Acceptance of Exile. Retrieved August 2022, from https://library.brown.edu/create/modernlatinamerica/chapters/chapter-11-brazil/moments-in-brazilian-history-2/dom-pedro-iis-acceptance-of-exile/

Racists Gallery. (2020, December 14). Diogo Feijó. Retrieved August 2022, from https://galeriaderacistas.com.br/en/diogo-feijo/

Ramerini, M. (2022, January 28). The Dutch in Brazil. Retrieved August 2022, from https://www.colonialvoyage.com/dutch-in-brazil/

Reference.com. (2020, May 27). Why did Europeans want a new route to Asia? Retrieved August 2022, from https://www.reference.com/history/did-europeans-want-new-route-asia-c8e82c4b27a1898b

Romero, S. (2014, March 28). Discoveries Challenge beliefs on humans' arrival in the Americas. Retrieved August 2022, from https://www.nytimes.com/2014/03/28/world/americas/discoveries-challenge-beliefs-on-humans-arrival-in-the-americas.html

Romero, S. (2016, December 14). A 'Stonehenge,' and a mystery, in the Amazon. Retrieved August 2022, from https://www.nytimes.com/2016/12/14/world/americas/brazil-amazon-megaliths-stonehenge.html

Rough and Polished. (2013, October 2). Amsterdam and the Culture of Diamonds. Retrieved August 2022, from https://www.rough-polished.com/en/expertise/82406.html

Royalty.nu. (2022). Royalty in Brazil. Retrieved August 2022, from http://www.royalty.nu/America/Brazil.html

Salon. (2007, May 2). How Portugal screwed up Brazil. Retrieved August 2022, from https://www.salon.com/2007/05/02/brazilian_gold/

Schmitz, P. I. (1987). Prehistoric Hunters and Gatherers of Brazil. *Journal of World Prehistory,* 1(1), 53–126. http://www.jstor.org/stable/25800520

Schneider, Ronald Milton, Minkel, C.W. and Leite, Aureliano. (2022, April 10). São Paulo. Retrieved August 2022, from https://www.britannica.com/place/Sao-Paulo-Brazil

Silva, J., & Penna, E. J. (1965). *História Do Brasil.* National Company.

Sowerbutts, L. (2019, October 17). Alluvial and Placer Mineral Deposits. Retrieved August 2022, from https://www.geologyforinvestors.com/alluvial-and-placer-mineral-deposits/

Survival International. (2022). Brazilian Indians. Retrieved August 2022, from https://www.survivalinternational.org/tribes/brazilian

Svisero, D., Shigley, J. E., & Weldon, R. (2017). Brazilian diamonds: A historical and recent perspective. Retrieved August 2022, from https://www.gia.edu/gems-gemology/spring-2017-brazilian-diamonds

TimeMaps. (2021, May 19). History of Brazil, 1648 CE. Retrieved August 2022, from https://www.timemaps.com/history/brazil-1648ad/

U.S. Library of Congress. (2022). The Military Republic, 1964-85. Retrieved August 2022, from http://countrystudies.us/brazil/18.htm

U.S. Library of Congress. (2022). The Post-Vargas Republic, 1954-64. Retrieved August 2022, from http://countrystudies.us/brazil/17.htm

U.S. Library of Congress. (2022). The Regency Era, 1831-40. Retrieved August 2022, from http://countrystudies.us/brazil/12.htm

U.S. Library of Congress. (2022). The Second Empire, 1840-89. Retrieved August 2022, from http://countrystudies.us/brazil/13.htm

Williamson, C. E. (2015, February 18). Brazilian indigenous populations grow quickly after first contact devastation. Retrieved August 2022, from https://news.mongabay.com/2015/02/brazilian-indigenous-populations-grow-quickly-after-first-contact-devastation/

Worrall, S. (2021, May 03). Cannibalism-the ultimate taboo-is surprisingly common. Retrieved August 2022, from https://www.nationalgeographic.com/culture/article/cannibalism-common-natural-history-bill-schutt

Worrall, S. (2021, May 03). Tracking a mystery: When and how the first Americans arrived. Retrieved August 2022, from https://www.nationalgeographic.com/science/article/when-and-how-did-the-first-americans-arrive--its-complicated-?loggedin=true

Www.encyclopedia.com. (2018, May 18). Tobacco Industry. Retrieved August 2022, from https://www.encyclopedia.com/history/united-states-and-canada/us-history/tobacco-industry

Www.encyclopedia.com. (2019). Mazombos. Retrieved August 2022, from https://www.encyclopedia.com/humanities/encyclopedias-almanacs-transcripts-and-maps/mazombos

Zimmerman, R., Dr. (2020). An introduction to colonial Brazil. Retrieved August 2022, from https://www.khanacademy.org/humanities/art-americas/new-spain/colonial-brazil/a/an-introduction-to-colonial-brazil

Made in United States
North Haven, CT
10 July 2023

38774542R00070